THE TOP 160
SUPERFOODS

A cook's directory of power foods and their benefits, shown in over 200 photographs

AUDREY DEANE

southwater

This edition is published by Southwater,
an imprint of Anness Publishing Ltd,
Blaby Road, Wigston,
Leicestershire LE18 4SE;
info@anness.com

www.southwaterbooks.com; www.annesspublishing.com

If you like the images in this book and would like to investigate using them for publishing, promotions or advertising, please visit our website www.practicalpictures.com for more information.

Publisher: Joanna Lorenz
Editorial Director: Helen Sudell
Project Editor: Melanie Hibbert
Design: Nigel Partridge
Production Controller: Wendy Lawson

© Anness Publishing Ltd 2013

A CIP catalogue record for this book is available from the British Library.

Previously published as part of a larger volume,
The Encyclopedia of Superfoods

Important: pregnant women, the elderly, the ill and very young children should avoid recipes using raw or lightly cooked eggs.

Publisher's Note:
Although the advice and information in this book are believed to be accurate and true at the time of going to press, neither the authors nor the publisher can accept any legal responsibility or liability for any errors or omissions that may have been made nor for any inaccuracies nor for any loss, harm or injury that comes about from following instructions or advice in this book.

THE TOP 160
SUPERFOODS

Contents

Introduction

For thousands of years, civilizations have recognized the fact that various foods have different effects on our body, and that our diet has an important role to play in keeping us healthy. In ancient times, the Chinese, Greeks, Romans and Egyptians all understood that diet was an essential part of our well-being, and this knowledge informed many of the food customs and traditions that are still in evidence today.

The scientific study of food and its impact on health is well documented and dates back to the 18th century, when learned men and physicians began to travel the world studying the effects of nutritional deficiencies. One of the best-known breakthroughs was the realization that citrus fruits could prevent scurvy among sailors. However, it was not until the late 1920s, with the discovery of vitamin C, that people fully understood what it was in the citrus fruits that kept the disease at bay. By this time the number of researchers working in the field of nutritional science had exploded, and this 'Golden Age' of nutritional analysis led to the discovery of many of the basic factors required to maintain a healthy diet and prevent disease.

Below: Drink fresh fruit juice to contribute to your 'five-a-day' intake.

This research has continued into the modern day and, with the advent of highly sophisticated techniques and scientific procedures, many new findings are being made all the time. Unfortunately, the claims of some supposed 'superfoods', traditionally well-regarded in areas such as Chinese herbal, Ayurvedic and homeopathic medicine, have not stood up to modern scientific scrutiny.

It is worth noting that, although widely used, the word 'superfood' is not a legally recognized term. The European Union are now reviewing a whole spectrum of nutritional claims with the ultimate aim of publishing a list of credible declarations.

Whether the term 'superfood' will ever become legally recognized is debatable, but it is now commonly used to describe foods with a beneficial nutritional content.

Food for Health

There are a wide range of substances found in foods, sometimes termed phytonutrients, or phytochemicals, that are reported to have beneficial effects on health and well-being. The term 'phyto' means from plants, but animal-derived foods are now emerging that are also being included in the superfoods family. While each superfood generally contains a particular beneficial nutrient, it is very important to emphasize that these benefits can't be fully exploited unless they are eaten as part of a healthy balanced diet. They will not mitigate the adverse effects of a poor diet and lifestyle, so it's no good eating a diet high in saturated fat, taking no exercise and smoking, then eating a handful of blueberries and a bowl of porridge and thinking everything is going to be just fine.

Foods High in Antioxidants:

Antioxidant-rich foods, such as blueberries, goji berries, oranges and tomatoes, are usually part of the fruit

Above: Antioxidant-rich raspberries taste great in a smoothie.

and vegetable family and indeed were probably the first group of foods to be given the name superfoods. Antioxidants are thought to be crucial for our well being due to their powerful ability to 'mop up' free radicals that circulate around the body. These free radicals may be introduced from external factors such as through smoking or come from our own bodily processes. It is thought that an excess of these may be a factor in the occurrence of cancer and this may be why a diet high in fruit and vegetables could help us to avoid a third of all cancers. Many vitamins have antioxidant activity, such as vitamin A (retinol), vitamin C (ascorbic acid) and vitamin E (tocopherol) as well as some minerals, including selenium. All have a vital role to play in keeping potentially harmful substances in check and preventing them from causing diseases such as cancer.

Foods High in Flavonoids: These

substances, also known as polyphenols, are found in food and drinks such as tea, red wine and chocolate. Flavonoids have some antioxidant activity, but it is their role in cell signalling that is the basis for their reported health benefits. Studies have shown that they are able to regulate the cell signals and can affect cell growth, thus possibly influencing cancer incidence. These compounds could also reduce the risk of coronary heart disease and atherosclerosis, a condition where the arteries become clogged with fatty deposits such as cholesterol. Flavonoids may also have beneficial effects in brain disorders such as Alzheimer's and Parkinson's disease.

Foods High in Phytosterols:
These important compounds, found in wheatgerm and brown rice, may have the ability to lower blood cholesterol levels by altering the way it is metabolized by the body. Found in plant cells, phytosterols are the plant equivalent of animal cholesterol. The highest concentrations of phytosterols are found in grain and bean oils and lower amounts are found in fruit and vegetables.

Foods High in Isoflavones and Phytoestrogens:
These substances, present in foods such as soya beans, alfalfa and chickpeas, show strong antioxidant activity and also provide dietary oestrogens that have beneficial effects on some of the hormonal systems of the body. These include helping to control blood cholesterol and reducing negative effects of the menopause such as osteoporosis. They may also have a role to play in protecting the body against cancers such as those of the breast and prostate.

Foods High in Dietary Fibre:
The general population does not eat enough fibre, yet fibre is important because it helps the body with many key functions. It can help improve your gastrointestinal health and glucose metabolism, helping those suffering from Type II Diabetes. It can help reduce coronary heart disease risk factors by reducing bad blood fats and hypertension, and also

reduce the risk of developing some cancers. Eating a higher fibre diet makes us feel fuller for longer after a meal so can help with weight control.

Foods High in Healthy Fats: Fat has had a lot of bad press in recent years, with people striving for a low-fat diet. We now recognize that though many of us would benefit from lower-fat diets, the type of fats we are consuming is equally important. Generally, we should be eating fewer saturated varieties and more of the healthy fats – mono-unsaturated and polyunsaturated fat. These healthy fats, present in foods such as olive oil, oily fish, flaxseed and walnuts, are important as they influence how we control cholesterol in our bodies, an excess of which can cause problems such as narrowing of arteries, which leaves us prone to heart attack and stroke.

Healthy omega-3 fats (part of the polyunsaturated fat family) are particularly important as they have many unique roles to play in the body, ranging from brain structure and function to potentially reducing excessive inflammatory reactions such as rheumatoid arthritis.

Above: For optimum nutrition, eat a good variety of fruit and vegetables.

Variety is Key
Many other compounds have been discovered in foods and some of these are very specific in their effect on the body. What this all points to is that it is best to eat as many different types of food as possible to gain the most benefit. The value of knowing about the different types of superfoods is in enabling you to understand those foods that may be of the most benefit to you, depending on your specific needs, when included in your balanced diet. Remember to always consult with a medical professional first, especially if you suffer from chronic illness or are on prescription medicines, as a change in diet may do more harm than good.

The basic elements of a healthy diet and lifestyle are outlined in the introductory section. Following this chapter about healthy living, a detailed directory provides key information for some of the most nutrient-packed superfoods known. The directory is followed by 150 mouthwatering, nutrient-rich recipes, each containing at least one or more superfood ingredients.

Balancing good health and lifestyle

A healthy, balanced diet should be based primarily on the regular consumption of unrefined complex carbohydrate-rich starchy foods and fruit and vegetables, with a slightly lower contribution from protein-rich foods and dairy products and a restricted intake of foods high in fat, salt and sugar. These proportions should provide your body with the energy and essential nutrients that it needs to maintain optimum health.

Carbohydrates

Foods rich in carbohydrates, such as bread, pasta, potatoes and sugar, provide the body with its main energy source. The body breaks down the more starchy foods such as bread, rice and potatoes into simple sugars such as glucose, which can then be used as energy. About one third of our food intake should come from wholegrain starchy foods. This will provide about half of the body's energy requirements. Starchy foods often contain other useful nutrients including protein, vitamins and minerals.

Sugar is sometimes termed an 'empty food' or 'empty calories' as it has no nutrient value other than energy and should be restricted by those trying to control their weight. It is useful in sport and for diabetics, who need a quick energy boost, but this is short-lived as the body counteracts this rise in blood sugar with the release of the hormone insulin. For most of us, therefore, it is healthier to eat carbohydrate foods that release energy much more slowly and don't induce the spikes in blood sugar levels that we then have to process. The measure of how fast sugar is released from a food is known as its GI (Glycaemic Index) value; the fastest being pure sugar at 100 and the lowest being some of the wholegrain, high-fibre foods, such as oats, wholegrain breads, brown rice and pulses. Foods with a low carbohydrate content, for example milk, meat, eggs and green vegetables, also have low GI values so release their energy gradually.

Fibre

Another type of carbohydrate, fibre is largely indigestible by the body and its importance in the diet cannot be underestimated. There are two types of fibre: soluble and insoluble. Insoluble fibre, such as in brown rice and pasta, is associated with improving the bulk of stools as it absorbs water. This prevents constipation and could be a factor in reducing cancer of the bowel and colon. Soluble fibre, as is found in apples, oats and lentils, is quite different as it can actually be partially digested in the lower intestine and fermented by the gut's bacteria. This produces beneficial compounds that are absorbed back into the body and these help to keep the gut healthy. Wholegrain foods, like some cereals and vegetables, are high in fibre and have the added benefit of retaining the nutrient-rich germ often removed in manufacturing.

Proteins

These are essential for growth, repair and maintenance of every cell in the body. They provide the building blocks to make muscle, hormones and enzymes, and are crucial in many

THE MAIN FOOD GROUPS
The pie chart below illustrates the proportions of the five main food groups that you should be aiming to eat each day.

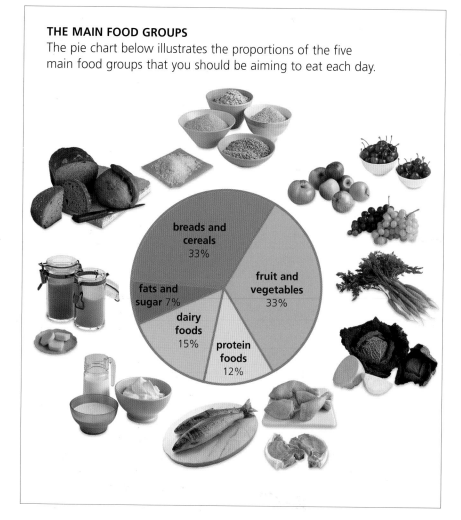

breads and cereals
33%

fruit and vegetables
33%

fats and sugar 7%

dairy foods
15%

protein foods
12%

metabolic processes. Proteins are made up of amino acid units, of which there are 20. Most can be made by the body itself, however eight cannot; these are termed 'essential' as we have to get them from our food. Generally, animal sources of proteins such as meat, fish and eggs contain all of the essential amino acids, whereas most plant sources are lacking in one or more of them. Some examples of plant foods containing the full complement of amino acids are soya, quinoa and buckwheat. It is important to eat a variety of protein foods to ensure that we get all of the essential amino acids that we need.

Fats and Oils

Given the amount of bad press that it gets, it may surprise you to learn that fat is essential in the diet. Modern dietary advice concentrates on the type of fats we eat. Fat is the most concentrated form of energy, releasing twice as many calories as the same amounts of carbohydrate and protein, which is why eating too much tends to make us overweight. However, fat also contains the vital fat-soluble vitamins A, D and E and provides us

Below: Cook with healthier vegetable oils rather than butter.

FAT TYPES
Saturated
Meat, dairy, lard
Unsaturated
Monounsaturated: olive oil, groundnut oil, sesame oil
Polyunsaturated: rapeseed oil, soya oil, fish oil

with essential fatty acids, all of which are critical to our good health.

Diets high in saturated fats have been associated with raised blood cholesterol and an increased risk of heart disease, a fact corroborated by the World Health Organization (WHO), which recommends avoiding saturated fat in order to reduce the risk of a cardiovascular disease. The body of evidence has changed opinions about dietary cholesterol and its effect on blood cholesterol. While we used to think that eating cholesterol-containing foods such as eggs and prawns could raise our blood cholesterol, we now know that the biggest influence is the amount of saturated fats that we eat. People whose diets are high in saturated fats are more likely to have raised levels

Below: Lean meat and fish are high in protein and low in saturated fat.

Above: Drink plenty of water after exercising to prevent dehydration.

of cholesterol. Unsaturated fats such as some seed oils help to restore the correct balance of the two types of cholesterol found in the body. HDL cholesterol is good, whereas LDL cholesterol is bad as high levels of LDL cholesterol are associated with an increased risk of heart disease.

Water

Our body is approximately 50 per cent water, so it is important to replenish our supplies. We continuously lose water through breathing, perspiring and getting rid of waste products. We need water to keep us cool, for transporting nutrients around the body in the blood and ensuring that the kidneys can function properly. Fluid can be taken in through our food as well as through drinking liquids, and we

---

KEEP HUNGER PANGS AT BAY
It is especially important at the start of the day to eat foods that have a low GI so that they release energy slowly and stop you from feeling hungry before lunchtime. Try eating a bowl of porridge or wholegrain cereal for breakfast.

need 1.5–2 litres/2½–3½ pints a day. The body is actually very good at telling us whether we are dehydrated: our urine becomes darker as our kidneys re-absorb more water back into the body, we become thirsty and we may get headaches.

Problems arise when we fail to recognize these signs and just feel unwell. Tea and coffee, while being mild diuretics, do contribute to fluid intake as does the food that we eat, so it doesn't all have to come from pure water. It is especially important to keep an eye on our fluid intake during hot weather or when we do exercise, as we lose water more rapidly and in greater quantities.

Vitamins and Minerals

Since our bodies have to get what we need from our diets, vitamins and minerals are essential to us. Foods may be rich in some vitamins and minerals but deficient in others, so it is important to eat a varied diet to ensure that we get the full range. However, vitamins and minerals can also interact with each other with positive and negative effects. We need adequate vitamin C to help iron absorption; conversely, excessive dietary calcium can reduce the

---

EAT A RAINBOW

Remember to include as many food colours in your diet as you possibly can. This chart shows you the nutrients offered by the different colour groups.

Yellow/Orange	Orange/Red	Red/Purple/Blue	Green	White
Food sources:				
Carrots	Oranges	Blueberries	Spinach	Garlic
Sweet potato	Tomatoes	Cranberries	Kale	Leeks
Cantaloupe melon	Watermelon	Red grapes	Broccoli	Onion
Pumpkin	Pink grapefruit	Elderberries	Greens	
Super nutrients:				
B-carotene	Lycopene	Anthocyanins	Lutein	Allicin
A-carotene	B-carotene	Betacyanins	Zeaxanthin	
	Z-carotene	Proanthocyanidins	B-carotene	
			Chlorophyll	

---

absorption of zinc and iron. Some vitamins, like the B group and C, are water-soluble and need to be eaten every day as we cannot store them, whereas the fat-soluble vitamins A, D and E can be stored in the liver.

Fruit and vegetables are an excellent source of vitamins and minerals as well as many other fabulous nutrients. According to the World Health Organization (WHO), we should be eating at least 400g (or approximately five portions) of fruit and vegetables a day. This can include dried and canned fruit and vegetables, as well

Below: Stave off hunger pangs by snacking on antioxidant-rich grapes.

Below: Slow-energy releasing porridge is a great way to start the day.

as fruit juice and smoothies. The WHO estimates that a low vegetable and fruit intake is one of the top ten risk factors for mortality in the world, and eating sufficient amounts could save 2.7 million lives per year. The key to getting this right is to eat as many different types of fruit and vegetable as possible. The easiest way to do this is to use colour as a guide and aim to eat a rainbow of variety. Many of the powerful phytonutrients in fruit and vegetables contribute to the food's colour, and by consuming a variety of colours you can ensure that you take in a healthy range of these nutrients. All of the superfoods in this book can make valuable contributions to health, especially when a wide variety are included in the diet. Many of the recipes in this book use combinations of these foods to help you achieve this.

Sugar

This comes in many different guises – natural, added, white, brown, corn syrup and invert. Though most of us should eat less of it, sugar in foods can be a useful energy source, particularly when it encourages the consumption of foods rich in other useful nutrients, such as fruit. There is no benefit from choosing naturally occurring sugars such as cane sugar or honey over regular table sugar.

REDUCING SUGAR AND SALT
• Slowly reduce how much sugar you add to your tea or coffee until you wean yourself off it.
• Gradually mix more unsweetened cereal with your sugary favourite cereal to get used to less sugar at breakfast.
• Reduce how much salt you add to vegetables during the cooking process.
• Choose 'no added salt and sugar' foods.
• Don't put salt on the table.

From a nutritional or chemical viewpoint, they are very similar, with no nutritional value other than providing energy (calories). Sugar intake should be limited as it is highly cariogenic, which means that bacteria in the mouth convert the sugar to acids that cause tooth decay. This is why fruit juice, which contains a lot of natural sugars, should be drunk in moderation.

Salt
Eating too much salt can increase your blood pressure, which, in turn, puts you at greater risk of suffering

Below: Include as much variety of colour in your diet as possible.

from heart disease or stroke. We can all reduce how much we add to our cooking, but it is more difficult to limit our intake from pre-prepared foods, including ready meals, which are estimated to provide around 75 per cent of the salt that we eat. Our natural 'taste' for salt can be reduced as we get used to eating less by limiting our intake of salt-rich foods, including ham, bacon, sausages, cheese, salty snacks, soups, canned vegetables, ready meals and takeaway food.

Healthy Diet and Lifestlye
The best tips for an improved lifestyle are to take regular exercise, maintain the correct weight, eat little and often throughout the day, rest and sleep well, avoid alcohol and stop smoking.

For a healthier diet, try to eat more carbohydrate-rich foods, especially wholegrain types, eat more fruit and vegetables, consume more fish, cut down on sugar, salt and saturated fat, drink plenty of fluids, and do not skip breakfast. Remember to boost your diet with superfoods and include as many colours as you can.

Above: Fruit, vegetables and juices all contribute to our water intake.

ANTIOXIDANT STRENGTH AND ORAC SCORES
The antioxidant strength of a certain food can be determined using the ORAC (oxygen radical absorption capacity) score system. This gives an indication of how well the antioxidants in a certain food can prevent oxidation and neutralize the potentially harmful effects of free radicals. The foods with the highest scores include acai berries, blueberries, cranberries and artichoke hearts, as well as beans such as kidney, red and pinto. Spices also have exceptionally high ORAC values, but as they are consumed in such small quantities, they do not contribute significantly to the diet. While still to be scientifically proven, it is thought that neutralizing free radicals can help to minimize age-related degeneration and disease.

Healthy cooking

How we cook, prepare and store food can impact on its nutritional value. Some nutrients become more useful, or bio-available, to us through cooking, whereas some nutrients become less bio-available to us, or are destroyed. All food degrades over time from the moment that it is harvested, through the supply chain and to the shop or supermarket where we buy it. Whenever possible, we should buy food that looks fresh, is in good condition and is not damaged.

Good Storage
For fresh foods, the key is to keep the 'chill chain' going, so letting food warm up and get cold again is not good for the nutritional quality or safety of foods. Transport refrigerated food home as soon as possible and place in the fridge. For frozen foods, it is the freezing process that puts the food in nutritional limbo, so if food is allowed to defrost, nutritional quality starts to decline. For store-cupboard foods, it is important to store them in a cool dry place away

Below: Decant foods from packaging into sealable jars to retain freshness.

from strong smells such as cleaning fluids, as some foods can absorb these and become tainted. Some store-cupboard foods need to be kept in a dark place to slow fat rancidity; this is especially true of nuts, seeds and oils. Highly unsaturated oils, such as flaxseed oil and walnut oil, should be kept in the fridge as the cool temperature slows rancidity. Fruit and vegetables should be kept in a cool place and out of any plastic covering that may encourage mould growth. If you spot damaged or mouldy fruit or vegetables, remove them immediately otherwise they can contaminate the other foods and speed up spoilage.

To Cook or Not to Cook?
It is true that some nutrients are lost during cooking, however some nutrients actually become more bio-available. The chopping and peeling and cooking of many fruit and vegetables releases nutrients from the cellular structure. Sometimes cooking in a little oil can help to release nutrients from the food, such as

Below: Cook carrots in just a little oil to maximize their nutrient levels.

Above: Chop up fresh greens to make them more digestible.

the beta-carotene from carrots or the antioxidant lycopene from tomatoes. Conversely, vitamin C and some B-vitamins are destroyed by heat and so eating some raw fruit and vegetables may be beneficial.

Healthy Cooking Techniques
When cooking with oil, always try to use sparingly. Grill and dry-fry foods rather than using the deep fat fryer or lots of oil. Try crushing whole spices and then dry-frying them as this releases the flavour volatiles from the spices and makes them more digestible. Many vitamins are destroyed by high cooking temperatures or by boiling in water, so steam vegetables where possible to prevent the water-soluble vitamins leaching into the water. If you do need to boil the vegetables, use as little water as possible, boil until just soft, and try to use the water to make a gravy or sauce.

Use non-stick cooking equipment where you can as this instantly cuts down on how much oil and fat you use in recipes. As well as the teflon-coated pans, baking tins (pans), grill (broiling) pans and trays that are widely available, you can now also buy many silicone bakeware products which are also non-stick.

Healthy Cooking Appliances

The most well-known and probably widely used time-saving appliance is the microwave. This versatile cooker is a feature of most modern kitchens and contributes to a healthier diet by reducing cooking times for produce such as fruit and vegetables. The added convenience of being able to defrost frozen foods more quickly means you can fill your freezer with unprocessed home cooking to enjoy when time is limited.

Recently some new appliances have appeared on the market with the specific aim of helping you to cook more healthily. These range from halogen ovens and high-tech steam cookers through to low-fat frying and grilling appliances. Some have very impressive features.

Halogen ovens: This compact yet versatile appliance is energy-efficient and offers healthy cooking options. It uses the intense heat of a halogen bulb while a fan circulates the air rapidly. Food can be cooked in half the time of conventional methods, and no added fats or oils are needed. Cooking options include roasting, baking, grilling and steaming.

Electric steam cookers: Using a water reservoir to generate the steam, these range from basic one-compartment rice-cooker-style units all the way through to very clever, multi-compartment machines, with different temperature zones that allow different steaming times. The benefits of steaming foods are mainly the reduced nutrient loss and improved texture of delicate foods such as fish and some vegetables. If you haven't space for an electric steam cooker, use a steamer pan over boiling water.

Electric low-fat grills: The healthy credentials are based on the fact that the grill (broiler) can cook the food while the fat drains away, either into the ridges of the griddle or into a drip

USEFUL EQUIPMENT FOR HEALTHY FOOD

- Steamer – ideal for cooking vegetables, as more vitamins are retained than with boiling. Also good for cooking fish.
- Liquidizer or blender – perfect for making smoothies and juices as well as for smoothing soups and sauces (great for hiding fruit and vegetables from children).
- Griddle pan – reduces the amount of fat used to cook meat and vegetables.
- Food processor – useful for pulverizing nuts and seeds and making breadcrumbs.

Right: A blender enables you to make a speedy, nutritious soup.

tray. Look out for grills with removable dishwasher-safe plates. If you don't want to buy an appliance, use your oven grill with a wire rack.

Electric low-fat fryers: This does sound impossible, but products are being launched that use very small amounts of oil to cook food such as chips (French fries). This results in chips with less than 3 per cent fat content. The unit moves the food continuously ensuring an all over 'frying' effect without the oil being soaked up. Although pricey, the results are good.

Below: Chicken browns well and the fat drains away in a halogen oven.

Below: Steaming nutritious asparagus only takes a few minutes.

Good health through life

The principles of a good diet and lifestyle apply throughout our whole life and should become the norm rather than a faddy, short-term thing. Try to form good habits that will stay with you forever, and this will also have a benefit to all those around you, particularly children, who will hopefully adopt good habits too. Nutritional requirements change throughout our lives, and having a basic understanding of these will help you to meet your body's needs. The following guidelines give an overview of these changes, but remember that this broad advice is no substitute for individual advice given by a health professional such as a GP, nurse or dietician.

Pregnancy
Being pregnant puts a huge burden on the body so it is crucial for women who are planning to conceive to ensure that they are in optimum health:

Folic Acid: Helps protect against foetal abnormalities such as neural tube defects. Good sources include dark green leafy vegetables.

Below: Optimum nutrition is more important than ever during pregnancy.

Calcium and Vitamin D: Consider both of these together as they aid efficient absorption and utilization. Vitamin D is more important for women of Asian, African and Middle Eastern origin, as these women find it harder to get the vitamin D from sunlight, and have an increased risk of the baby contracting rickets. Good food sources of vitamin D are eggs and oily fish, while calcium-rich foods include dairy products and green leafy vegetables.

Omega-3 Fatty Acids: Crucial building blocks for brain and eye tissue in the foetus, it is best to try to eat the fish form of omega-3, as the vegetarian sources, such as linseeds and some rapeseed oil, are not so easily used by the body. Good sources include oily fish and seafood. However, because of concerns over toxins, shark, marlin or swordfish should be avoided and tuna limited. For other oily fish such as salmon, herring and trout, up to two portions a week are recommended. It is also important to maintain your omega-3 intake after having your baby as this may help avoid post-natal depression.

Iron: Due to the increasing blood volume and the foetus laying down stores of iron that will see it through the first six months of life, pregnant women are at risk of anaemia. However, the body is able to cope with this by increasing the absorption rate of iron from food while mobilizing iron stores, provided the mother has sufficient iron stores initially. Eating plenty of foods rich in vitamin C will also aid this.

Fibre: Some women suffer from constipation during pregnancy, so it is important to eat lots of fruit, vegetables and wholegrains. This, coupled with good fluid intake, will help to alleviate the problem.

Foods to Avoid: Liver and liver products are best avoided due to the potentially toxic affects of vitamin A on the baby. Avoid unpasteurized products such as cheeses, milk and fresh mayonnaise. Avoid alcohol, especially in the first two trimesters. If you have allergies, try to avoid eating nuts to reduce the risk of a nut allergy in the baby.

Young Infants
Most health organizations currently recommend that a young baby is fed exclusively either breastmilk or formula up to the age of six months. Breastmilk is thought to be best, especially in the first few weeks of life, as many crucial antibodies which are important in building a healthy immune system and other protective factors are passed from mother to baby. By six months, the baby's body can adequately digest and metabolize food, which enables vital replenishment of nutritional stores.

Calcium and Vitamin D: The rapid growth rate of the skeleton ensures that calcium requirements are kept high. Babies need to have at least 600ml (1 pint) of milk a day up to 1 year. This then drops to about 350ml/12 fl oz.

Iron: Babies stock up on their iron stores from the mother in the last trimester of pregnancy, and so long as the pregnancy is full-term these stores should last until 6–9 months of age. However, introducing cow's milk, low in iron, too early into a baby's diet will mean that these stores may run out sooner.

Vitamin C: This vitamin is essential to ensure optimal absorption of iron.

Omega 3: The baby's brain will still be growing rapidly and will need supplies of omega 3 to ensure that this is optimized.

Above: Children love vitamin-packed home-made fruit smoothies.

Toddlers and Young Children

The main challenges when ensuring good nutrition for toddlers and young children are their high energy and nutrient requirements, their small stomachs and their variable appetites. There are many growth spurts during this age range, leading to spikes in appetite, and this puts extra emphasis on those nutrients required to ensure optimal growth and development.

Particular nutrients to focus on are protein, iron, calcium and vitamins A, C and D. It will be entirely normal for children to become hungry between their three meals a day, and so highly nutritious snacks will be required to ensure good nutrition and to prevent them reaching for high-fat or sugary snacks such as crisps and chocolate.

Adolescents

The need for a good balanced diet during adolescence is essential to meet the body's growth requirements.

The main human growth spurt takes place now and energy and protein needs will be increased. This is particularly true of boys who may appear to be permanently hungry, and there is a risk that under-nutrition can inhibit growth. It is important that hunger pangs are alleviated with nutritious snacks throughout the day along with the normal meals. Breakfast cereals with milk are a good way to ensure that vitamin, mineral and calcium intakes are maintained.

Calcium: Calcium needs are high as bone growth is rapid, and much calcium is laid down in the bones that is essential for their life-long health. If calcium needs aren't met there is a greater risk of osteoporosis in later life.

Iron: Needed during growth for muscle and blood production, this is a key nutrient. It also becomes very important for girls as menstruation begins. Ensure vitamin C-rich foods are eaten to help absorption. This is particularly true for vegetarians, as iron from vegetables and pulses is more difficult to absorb.

Menopause

The main issue during the menopause is the increased risk of osteoporosis, a disease that affects up to 15 per cent of women aged 50. The best way to reduce the risk of developing osteoporosis is to ensure good bone density earlier in life and to reduce the rate of bone loss later in life.

Oestrogen helps to maintain bone density, so as oestrogen levels fall during the menopause, bones begin to lose calcium and the density decreases, heightening the risk of osteoporosis. It is important to ensure that calcium intakes are high at this time of life, and that vitamin D, which is integral to the way the body absorbs and uses calcium, is boosted.

Phytoestrogens are the plant version of our oestrogen so eating foods that contain these compounds could mimic their effect and may help to alleviate menopausal symptoms and preserve bone density.

Mature Adults

As we age, our bodies gradually wear out and we become less efficient at everything, including digestion and absorption of food. Since appetite also tends to decrease, food needs to be increasingly nutrient-rich as we age, to ensure all the body's nutritional needs are met.

Calcium and Vitamin D: Osteoporosis is a major cause of illness in people over the age of 50, and so it is vital to maintain a good calcium intake as well as to ensure that some skin is exposed to the sun for adequate production of vitamin D. One point to note is that glass does not let the important vitamin D-yielding sunrays through, so it is not sufficient to simply sit at a window. It is probably for this reason that vitamin D deficiency is a big problem in housebound elderly.

Iron: While iron requirements may not be higher in the elderly, there are many other factors that will interfere with iron absorption, including medication. Drinking tea during meal times can also reduce iron absorption, as the tannins bind with the iron to make it non-bioavailable. Ideally, tea should be drunk between meals and water or juice drunk with meals, so long as fluid intake is not then compromised.

Below: Keeping active will help to maintain good health as you mature.

Essential minerals and vitamins

Regular intake of a wide range of minerals and vitamins is essential for good health, and the vast majority can be found in many different foods. By frequently eating enough of the correct foods, including at least five portions of fruit and vegetables per day, most people should not need to take vitamin or mineral supplements. An exception to this is vitamin B12, which is only found in animal products and yeast extracts, so if you are vegan you may need to take this in supplement form. Try to eat a variety of different types and colours of produce each day, in particular brightly coloured and dark green fruit and vegetables, to ensure that you are obtaining as wide a range of nutrients and beneficial compounds as possible. This chart describes which foods are the richest sources, the role the mineral or vitamin plays in health maintenance, and the signs that may suggest a deficiency.

MINERAL	BEST SOURCES	ROLE IN HEALTH	DEFICIENCY
Calcium	Canned sardines (with bones), dairy products, green leafy vegetables, sesame seeds, dried figs and almonds.	Essential for building and maintaining strong bones and teeth, muscle function and the nervous system.	Deficiency is characterized by soft and brittle bones, osteoporosis, fractures and muscle weakness.
Chloride	Nuts, wholegrains, beans, peas, lentils, tofu and black tea.	Regulates and maintains the balance of fluids in the body.	Deficiency is rare.
Iodine	Seafood, seaweed and iodized salt.	Aids the production of hormones released by the thyroid gland.	Deficiency can lead to sluggish metabolism, and dry skin and hair.
Iron	Meat, offal, sardines, egg yolks, fortified cereals, leafy vegetables, dried apricots, tofu and cocoa.	Essential for healthy blood and muscles.	Deficiency is characterized by anaemia, fatigue and low resistance to infection.
Magnesium	Nuts, seeds, wholegrains, beans, peas, lentils, tofu, dried figs and apricots, and green vegetables.	Essential for healthy muscles, bones and teeth, normal growth, and nerves.	Deficiency is characterized by lethargy, weak bones and muscles, depression and irritability.
Manganese	Nuts, wholegrains, beans, lentils, brown rice, tofu and black tea.	Essential component of enzymes involved in energy production.	Deficiency is not characterized by any specific symptoms.
Phosphorus	Found in most foods, especially lean meat, poultry, fish, eggs, dairy products and nuts.	Essential for healthy bones and teeth, energy production and the absorption of many nutrients.	Deficiency is rare.
Potassium	Bananas, milk, beans, peas, lentils, nuts, seeds, whole grains, potatoes, fruit and vegetables.	Essential for water balance, regulating blood pressure, and nerve transmission.	Deficiency is characterized by weakness, thirst, fatigue, mental confusion and raised blood pressure.
Selenium	Meat, fish, citrus fruits, avocados, lentils, milk, cheese, Brazil nuts and seaweed.	Essential for protecting against free radical damage and may protect against cancer – an antioxidant.	Deficiency is characterized by reduced antioxidant protection.
Sodium	Found in most foods, but comes mainly from processed foods.	Essential for nerve and muscle function and body fluid regulation.	Deficiency is unlikely but can lead to dehydration and cramps.
Zinc	Lean meat, oysters, peanuts, cheese, wholegrains, seeds, beans, peas and lentils.	Essential for a healthy immune system, normal growth, wound healing, and reproduction.	Deficiency is characterized by impaired growth, slow wound healing, and loss of taste and smell.

VITAMIN	BEST SOURCES	ROLE IN HEALTH	DEFICIENCY
A (retinol in animal foods, betacarotene in plant foods)	Animal sources: liver, oily fish, milk, butter, cheese, egg yolks and margarine. Plant sources: orange-fleshed and dark green fruit and vegetables.	Essential for vision, bone growth, and skin and tissue repair. Beta-carotene acts as an antioxidant and protects the immune system.	Deficiency is characterized by poor night vision, dry skin and lower resistance to infection, especially respiratory disorders.
B1 (thiamin)	Lean meat (especially pork), wholegrain and fortified bread and cereals, brewer's yeast, potatoes, nuts, beans, peas, lentils and milk.	Essential for energy production, the nervous system, muscles, and heart. Promotes growth and boosts mental ability.	Deficiency is characterized by depression, irritability, nervous disorders, loss of memory. Common among alcoholics.
B2 (riboflavin)	Meat (especially liver), dairy, eggs, fortified bread and cereals, yeast extract and almonds.	Essential for energy production and for the functioning of vitamin B6 and niacin, as well as tissue repair.	Deficiency is characterized by lack of energy, dry cracked lips, numbness and itchy eyes.
Niacin (nicotinic acid, also called B3)	Lean meat, fish, beans, peas, lentils, potatoes, fortified breakfast cereals, wheatgerm, nuts, milk, eggs, peas, mushrooms, green leafy vegetables, figs and prunes.	Essential for healthy digestive system, skin and circulation. It is also needed for the release of energy.	Deficiency is unusual, but characterized by lack of energy, depression and scaly skin.
B6 (piridoxine)	Lean meat, fish, eggs, wholegrain cereals, brown rice, nuts and cruciferous vegetables, such as broccoli, cabbage and cauliflower.	Essential for assimilating protein and fat, for making red blood cells, and maintaining a healthy immune system.	Deficiency is characterized by anaemia, dermatitis and depression.
B12 (cyano-cobalamin)	Meat (especially liver), fish, milk, eggs, fortified breakfast cereals, cheese and yeast extract.	Essential for growth, formation of red blood cells and maintaining a healthy nervous system.	Deficiency is characterized by fatigue, increased risk of infection, and anaemia.
Folate (folic acid)	Offal, dark green leafy vegetables, wholegrain and fortified breakfast cereals, bread, nuts, beans, peas, lentils, bananas and yeast extract.	Essential for cell division; especially needed before conception and during pregnancy.	Deficiency is characterized by anaemia and appetite loss. Linked with neural defects in babies.
C (ascorbic acid)	Citrus fruit, melons, strawberries, tomatoes, broccoli, potatoes, (bell) peppers and green vegetables.	Essential for the absorption of iron, healthy skin, teeth and bones. Strengthens the immune system and helps to fight infection.	Deficiency is characterized by increased susceptibility to infection, fatigue, poor sleep and depression.
D (calciferol)	Mainly exposure to sunlight. Also liver, oily fish, eggs, fortified breakfast cereals and fortified dairy produce.	Essential for bone and tooth formation; helps the body to absorb calcium and phosphorus.	Deficiency is characterized by softening of the bones, muscle weakness and anaemia. Shortage in children can cause rickets.
E (tocopherols)	Oily fish, seeds, nuts, vegetable oils, eggs, wholemeal bread, avocados and spinach.	Essential for healthy skin, circulation, and maintaining cells – an antioxidant.	Deficiency is characterized by increased risk of heart attack, strokes and certain cancers.

SUPERFOODS DIRECTORY

This comprehensive guide lists all the main superfoods available, from the most vibrant and nutritious fruit and vegetables through to wholesome grains, pulses, nuts and seeds. The book finishes with the healthiest dairy, meat and fish choices. Included are details on the latest health benefits associated with each superfood and these, along with buying, cooking and storage tips, will help you to gain the most from these wonderful foods.

Fruit

Perhaps the ultimate convenience food, most fruits can be simply washed and eaten and, because the nutrients are concentrated just below the skin, it is best to avoid peeling. Cooking fruit reduces some valuable vitamins and minerals, so, if you can, eat it raw. Fruit is an excellent source of energy and provides valuable fibre and antioxidants, which are said to reduce the risk of heart disease and certain cancers. Thanks to modern farming methods and efficient transportation, most fruit is available all year round, although it is generally best when home-grown, organically produced and in season.

ORCHARD FRUITS

These refreshing fruits have a long history spanning thousands of years, and offer an incredible range of colours and flavours. Orchard fruits include many favourites, from crisp, juicy apples, which are available all year round, to luscious, fragrant apricots – a popular summer fruit.

Apples

The list of apple varieties is vast, with over 7,500 known cultivars, although only a fraction are in widespread commercial use. Some of the most well-liked eating varieties are Cox's Orange Pippin, Granny Smith, Gala, Braeburn, and Golden and Red Delicious. The most familiar cooking apple is the Bramley, with its thick, shiny, green skin and tart flesh. It is perfect for baking, or as the basis of apple sauce. Less well-known varieties, many of which have a short season, are often available from farmers' markets or farm shops. 'An apple a day keeps the doctor away' is a well-known adage, which is actually corroborated by scientific evidence as well as by tradition. Apples, while relatively low in vitamins and minerals compared to some other fruit, do have high levels of phenolic phytonutrients which

Above: Try to eat apples unpeeled as most nutrients are just under the skin.

have powerful antioxidant properties. The most predominant one is quercetin, which has been shown to have protective effects against cancer and heart disease by reducing cancer cell proliferation and reducing cell oxidative stress. Other compounds such as the catechins and epicatechin help to reduce fat by increasing oxidation, and in combination with the fibre content have been shown to reduce 'bad' LDL cholesterol levels. Most apples are stored after harvest

AN APPLE A DAY

Numerous studies have shown that eating apples regularly could reduce harmful LDL cholesterol in the body. In France, 30 middle-aged men and women were asked to add 2–3 apples a day to their diet for a month. By the end of the month, 80 per cent of the group showed reduced cholesterol levels, and in half of the group the drop was more than 10 per cent. Additionally, the level of good HDL cholesterol went up. Pectin, a soluble fibre found particularly in apples, is believed to be the magic ingredient.

BAKED APPLES

Baking is a simple and nutritious method of cooking apples. Use either large cooking varieties such as Bramley or eating apples such as golden delicous or gala.

1 Preheat the oven to 180°C/350°F/Gas 4. Remove the core of the apples, then score the skin around the circumference to prevent the skin bursting. Place the apples in a baking dish with a little water.

2 Fill the cavity of each apple with a mixture of dark brown sugar, dried fruit and nuts. Top each apple with a knob (pat) of butter. Place in the pre-heated oven and bake for approximately 40 minutes or until the apples are soft.

in controlled atmospheres in order to slow ripening, but this does not appear to affect the levels or activity of these beneficial phytonutrients. The skins of red apples also contain proanthocyanidin componds, which are part of the flavonoid family. These are important in cell-signalling processes and can help to reduce coronary heart disease risk.

Apples are delicious when they are eaten raw with their skin on, where the highest concentrations of these phenolic phytochemicals are found. Lower levels are found in the flesh and when apple juice is produced the concentrations drop even lower to around 10 per cent of the original apple. So, to maximize the benefits, keep the skin on where you can, cook apples over a low heat with little or no water and keep the lid on.

Pears

The humble pear has been popular for thousands of years and was extensively cultivated by both the Greeks and the Romans. Pears come into their own in the late summer and autumn with the arrival of the new season's crops. Favourites include green and brown-skinned Conference; Williams (Bartlett), with its thin, yellow skin and sweet, soft flesh; plump Comice, which has a pale yellow skin with a green tinge.

There are also more unusual pears such as the Asian pear, which has an uncharacteristic round shape and is particularly high in fibre. Like certain apples, some types of pear are good for cooking, others are best eaten raw, and a few varieties fit happily into both camps.

Pears can be used in both sweet and savoury dishes; they are excellent in salads, and can be baked, poached in syrup, and used in pies and tarts. They are less likely to cause allergic reactions, so make a perfect weaning food for babies when cooked and puréed. This also makes them a useful food when following an exclusion diet to establish which

Above: Pears are a good source of vitamin C, fibre and potassium.

foods may be causing an allergy or intolerance. Pears are often one of the first foods introduced back into the diet. Despite their high water content, the fruit contains useful amounts of vitamin C, and they are high in both soluble and insoluble fibre and potassium.

When buying, choose firm, plump fruit that are just slightly under-ripe. Pears can ripen in a day or so and then they pass their peak very quickly and become woolly or squashy. To tell if a pear is ripe, feel around the base of the stalk, where it should give slightly when gently pressed, but the pear itself should be firm.

Apricots

The best fresh apricots are sunshine gold in colour and full of juice. They are delicious baked or used raw in salads. An apricot is at its best when truly ripe; if the velvet flesh yields a little when gently pressed you know it is ready. Immature fruits are hard and tasteless, and never seem to ripen properly and attain the right level of sweetness. Apricots are rich in vitamin C and vitamin A, which is essential for good vision, as well as beta-carotene, a closely related substance that has strong antioxidant activity and could be helpful in reducing heart disease and cancer incidence.

Apricots are widely available dried, but this preserving method does involve sulphating the fresh apricot in order to keep the golden colour. So, if you are allergic or sensitive to sulphites, buy organic ones as no sulphites are used during the drying process which explains their dark brown colour. Dried apricots are more concentrated in nutrients weight for weight versus fresh, and are a good source of calcium and iron. They are a great healthy snack that counts as another portion of fruit, and are popular with children.

Below: Fresh, ripe apricots smell wonderfully fragrant.

Plums

Ranging in colour from pale yellow to dark, rich purple, plums come in many different varieties, although only a few are available in shops. As indicated by their rich colours, plums contain anthocyanin pigments. These include phytochemicals such as proanthocyanidins which are associated with reduced heart disease risk. They can be sweet and juicy or slightly tart; the latter are best cooked in pies and cakes, or made into a delicious jam. Sweet plums can be eaten as they are, and work well in fruit salads, or they can be puréed and combined with custard or yogurt to make a fruit fool. Plums should be just firm, and not too soft, with shiny, smooth skin that has a slight 'bloom'. Store ripe plums in the refrigerator. Unripe fruits can be kept at room temperature for a few days to ripen.

Prunes

These fruits are actually dried plums and this popular dried fruit has been used for centuries in the treatment of constipation. This is due to the combination of a high fibre content

Below: High levels of phytochemicals in plums help to fight heart disease.

and the presence of a natural laxative, which makes them particularly effective. They also have a notably high level of antioxidant activity, mainly due to the presence of polyphenols and flavonoids. It takes only three prunes to count as a portion of fruit towards the five fruit and vegetable portions a day that are recommended. Prune juice is also popular, and the juicing process does not remove the natural laxatives or the soluble fibre so it is still as effective as dried prunes. Prunes also have a low GI value, making them excellent as a healthy snack that provides slow release energy. Chop up some prunes in your porridge, or just carry a few in a small bag to ease those mid-morning hunger pangs.

Cherries

There is nothing like devouring a bag of fresh ripe cherries, and knowing that these little gems are good for you is a great bonus. There are two types: sweet and sour. Sweet cherries such as the Bing cherry are best eaten raw, while the sour type, such as Morello, are best cooked. Choose firm, bright, glossy fruits that have

Below: Slow energy-releasing prunes are a good choice for breakfast.

Above: Sweet cherries make a great antioxidant-rich snack.

fresh, green stems. Discard any that are soft, or have split or damaged skin. Cherries contain Vitamin C and fibre, and more importantly, their deep red skins are a rich source of anthocyanins, which may have anti-cancer attributes as well as cardioprotective properties. The possible anti-cancer attributes of anthocyanins are currently one of the most heavily researched areas, as they are probably one of the most widely available phytonutrients in the general diet. Research is also ongoing research on the cell-signalling effects of anthocyanins and potential beneficial uses as an anti-inflammatory.

Quinces

Fragrant, with a thin yellow or green skin, these knobbly fruits, which can be either apple- or pear-shaped, are always cooked as they are unpleasant if eaten raw. Quinces are rich in soluble fibre and pectin, which means that they are not only good for you but are also excellent for making jams and jellies. In France and Spain, quinces are used to make a fruit paste that is delicious served with cheese. Fragrant quince flesh is also a lovely addition when cooking apple sauce. Always look for smooth ripe fruits that are not too soft.

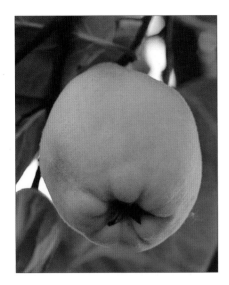

Above: High-fibre quince is delicious served with savoury dishes.

Quinces keep well and can be stored in a bowl in the kitchen or living room. They will fill the room with their aroma. They also help to calm the stomach and allay sickness.

RHUBARB
Technically a vegetable, and growing in colder climes, the fleshy stalks of the rhubarb plant are eaten as a fruit. They have an extremely tart flavour that really needs to be sweetened to make them more palatable, especially if it is being eaten for dessert. Rhubarb leaves are highly toxic, but the young pink tender stems cook in minutes and make a perfect pie or crumble filling, or a juicy compote to eat with yogurt or ice cream. Rhubarb is also a good non-dairy source of calcium, although the oxalate content does reduce its bioavailability somewhat. Due to its anthraquinone and fibre content, rhubarb is a good laxative to use if you are constipated, however, continual use causes problems for the colon. Chinese herbal medicine has used rhubarb and rhubarb root extract for many years for various intestinal complaints. It has been reported that rhubarb may have anti-cancer and anti-inflammatory properties, which may help to reduce

Above: A portion of dried fruit can count as one of your five-a-day.

blood pressure, but these research results have not been corroborated by further studies.

DRIED FRUIT
A useful concentrated source of energy and nutrients, dried fruit is higher in calories than fresh fruit, and packed with vitamins and minerals. This means that it contributes to the recommended fruit and vegetable target of five portions a day. The drying process boosts the levels of vitamin C, beta-carotene, potassium

and iron. Dried apricots are popular but dried apples, pears, bananas and pineapples are also available.

As dried fruits are so concentrated, a portion size for your five-a-day is surprisingly small. Just three dried apricots or prunes make up one portion size.

DRIED FRUIT TIPS
• Add a handful of your favourite dried fruits to your breakfast cereal for an energy-boosting start to the day.
• Keep a small snack bag of dried fruit in your bag for when you get an attack of those hunger pangs.
• Take dried fruit on a long car journey to stop you grazing on unhealthy snack foods such as crisps, cookies and sweets.
• Add your favourite dried fruit mix to bread, cakes, scones and cookies when baking.
• Add dried fruit to lunchboxes and picnics and keep some on hand for after-school snacks or a post-exercise lift.

Below: Choose thin, slender stems of rhubarb for the best flavour.

CITRUS FRUITS

Juicy and vibrant, citrus fruits, such as oranges, grapefruit, lemons and limes, are best known for their sweet, slightly sour juice, which is rich in vitamin C. They are invaluable in the kitchen for adding an aromatic acidity to many dishes, from soups and sauces to puddings and pies.

Here we concentrate on those citrus fruits that have a little more than just vitamin C to bring to the superfood arena.

Eating an orange a day should supply an adult's requirement for vitamin C, but citrus fruits also contain phosphorous, potassium, calcium, beta-carotene and fibre. Pectin, a soluble fibre found in the flesh and particularly in the membranes of citrus fruit, is known to reduce cholesterol levels. The fruits also contain flavanones, which not only have powerful antioxidant properties but are also thought to help reduce the risk of heart disease, neuro-degenerative disease and certain types of cancers.

Choosing Citrus Fruit

Look for plump, firm citrus fruit that feels heavy for its size, and has a smooth thin skin; this indicates that the flesh is juicy. Fruits with bruises, brown spots, green patches (or yellow patches on limes) and soft, squashy skin should be avoided, as should dry, wrinkled specimens. Citrus fruits can be kept at room temperature for a few days but if you want to keep them longer, they are best stored in the refrigerator and

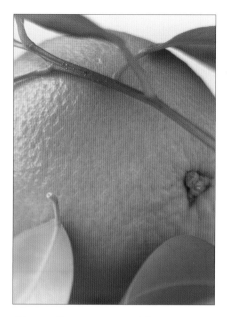

Above: Oranges are a rich source of vitamin C, pectin and folate.

eaten within two weeks. Alternatively, cut lengthways into segments and freeze. When required, just leave for five minutes at room temperature to defrost and they will be ready to use.

Oranges

Thin-skinned oranges tend to be the juiciest, and sweet varieties like Jaffa and Valencia are perfect eaten fresh. Seville, a sour orange, is cooked with sugar to make marmalade, which was the original way of preserving oranges. Famed for their vitamin C content, oranges are also a good source of pectin, a fibre found mainly in the skin around each segment, which has been shown to reduce 'bad' LDL cholesterol levels. Oranges are also a useful source of folate, which is essential if you are pregnant or are trying to get pregnant. A glass of freshly squeezed orange juice, while not retaining the pectin, is a good source of folate, thiamine and potassium and still counts as a portion of fruit. Oranges are also a useful source of flavanones such as hesperidin, which has been shown to strengthen blood vessels, and may play an important role in reducing heart disease risk and protecting

---

GRATING CITRUS RIND	CUTTING FINE STRIPS OR JULIENNE

1 For long, thin shreds of rind, use a zester. Scrape it along the surface of the fruit, applying firm pressure.

2 For finer shreds, use a grater. Rub the fruit over the fine cutters to remove the rind without any of the white pith.

1 Use a vegetable peeler to remove strips of orange rind. Make sure the white pith remains on the fruit.

2 Stack several strips of the citrus rind and, using a sharp knife, cut them into long, fine strips or julienne.

Above: Limes add sharpness and vitamin C to sweet or savoury dishes.

against neuro-degenerative diseases. Hesperidin is converted to hesperitin in the intestine, and this compound has neuro-protective properties as it is thought to reduce the damage caused by oxidation.

Lemons
Both the juice and the flesh of the lemon can be used to enliven vegetables, dressings, marinades, sauces and biscuits (cookies). Lemon juice can also be used to prevent some fruits and vegetables from discolouring when cut.

Also containing flavanones, in particular hesperidin, lemons are of interest to scientists researching ways of reducing neuro-degenerative risk. The best lemons should be deep yellow in colour, firm and heavy for their size, with no hint of green in the skin. A thin, smooth skin is indicative of juicy flesh.

CITRUS FRUIT TIP
Roll uncut citrus fruit firmly over a work surface or between your hands to extract the maximum amount of juice from the fruit.

GRAPEFRUIT WARNING
Some compounds present in grapefruit can interact with many prescribed drugs, reducing their effectiveness and causing other problems. If taking medication, consult with a pharmacist or medical professional before increasing grapefruit consumption.

Limes
Once considered to be rather exotic, limes are now widely available. The juice has a sharper flavour than that of lemons and if you substitute limes for lemons in a recipe, you will need to use less juice. Limes do contain the beneficial flavanones referred to earlier, but in slightly lower concentrations than oranges and lemons. This is also true of their vitamin C content. Limes are used widely in Asian cooking to flavour curries, marinades and dips. Chillies, coriander, garlic and ginger are all natural partners. Try to avoid limes with a yellowing skin as this is a sign of deterioration.

Pink and Ruby Grapefruits
The flesh of the grapefruit ranges in colour from vivid pink and ruby red to white; the pink and red varieties are sweeter and are of particular interest due to their lycopene content, which is responsible for their attractive colour. Lycopene, also found in tomatoes, is a carotenoid that has been studied extensively for its role in reducing the risk of prostate cancer in men. Many studies have shown that men whose diet is rich in lycopene show a significantly lower incidence of prostate cancer. Served juiced, halved or cut into slices, grapefruit traditionally provides a refreshing start to the day. The fruit also adds a tang to salads and makes a contrast to rich foods. Cooking or grilling mellows the tartness, but keep cooking times brief.

Above: Pink grapefruits taste sweeter than the yellow varieties.

BENEFITS OF VITAMIN C
Vitamin C and its health benefits are probably among the most researched areas in nutritional science. We know the body is unable to store vitamin C so it must rely on a daily intake from food. While found primarily in citrus fruits, vitamin C is also found in most fruit and vegetables – the highest concentrations are actually in kiwis and guavas.

A powerful antioxidant, vitamin C may help to reduce the risk of certain cancers such as of the stomach, mouth and lung. Evidence suggests that populations with vitamin C-rich diets have a reduced risk of strokes and coronary heart disease. This vitamin plays an important part in the synthesis of collagen, blood vessels and bone. It is also involved in the metabolism of cholesterol and can reduce harmful LDL cholesterol. Its role in preventing colds hasn't been scientifically proven, but it may reduce the severity.

BERRIES AND CURRANTS

These baubles of vivid red, purple and black are the epitome of summer and autumn, at the height of their season. Nowadays, these fruits are readily available all year round. Despite their distinctive appearance and flavour, berries and currants are interchangeable in their uses – jams, jellies, pies and tarts are the obvious choices. Berries are fabulous on their own or as combinations, and the benefits of including more of these in our diets cannot be ignored.

Strawberries

These are one of the favourite summer fruits and do not need any embellishment. Best served when juicy and ripe on their own, or with a

Below: Strawberries are a good source of manganese and vitamin C.

little cream or some natural yogurt. Wash gently and only just before serving, otherwise they will go mushy.

Strawberries contain a flavonoid called fisetin, which has been shown to notably improve brain function, and in one study improved the memory of rats. However, the equivalent amount of strawberries for humans would be approximately ten punnets a day, which even the most committed strawberry lover would struggle with. Fisetin is also an antioxidant and has been shown to have anti-cancer properties, and it is being researched for its effects as an anti-inflammatory for reducing allergic responses. The fisetin flavonoid is very heat-stable and does not appear to be destroyed by heat. It is well documented but often forgotten that strawberries are an excellent source of Vitamin C and are

FRUIT PURÉE

Soft berries are perfect for making uncooked fruit purées or coulis. Sweeten if the fruit is tart and add a splash of lemon juice to bring out the flavour.

1 To make a purée, place some raspberries, with lemon juice and icing (confectioners') sugar to taste, in a food processor or blender and pulse until smooth.

2 Press through a nylon sieve (strainer). Store in the refrigerator for up to two days.

also rich in manganese, which is an essential mineral for the maintenance of bone health and metabolism.

Raspberries

Soft and fragrant, raspberries are best served simply and unadulterated – maybe with a spoonful of natural (plain) yogurt. Those grown in Scotland are regarded as the best in the world. Raspberries are very fragile and require the minimum of handling, so wash only if really necessary. They are best eaten raw, as cooking can spoil their flavour and destroy vitamin C content. Raspberries are a rich source of

Above: Fresh raspberries on their own make a nutrient-rich dessert.

Above: Blackcurrants are tiny, but are packed full of vitamin C.

Above: Blueberries are bursting with cancer-fighting phytonutrients.

vitamin C and vitamin K, which is essential for blood clotting, and just like strawberries they are rich in manganese. Raspberries have one of the highest antioxidant strengths of all of the fruits; this is due to the combined effect of the high vitamin C content along with the anthocyanins and other flavonoids present in the berry. These powerful antioxidants prevent the harmful action of free radicals and may help to prevent degenerative brain diseases such as Alzheimer's. Research is being conducted into the benefits of antioxidant activity in cancer prevention and treatment. Studies into the fruit's anti-inflammatory properties have also shown promise. These factors, combined with a very high-fibre content, mean that raspberries pack a powerful nutrient punch.

Blackcurrants
As the intense dark colour suggests, these tiny berries are crammed full of anthocyanins, which have excellent antioxidant activity. Blackcurrants, like citrus fruits, are well known for their vitamin C content and you only need about 30g/1¼oz of them to get your daily requirement. As well as high

levels of anthocyanins and vitamin C, blackcurrants contain both soluble and insoluble fibre, important in maintaining good intestinal health, and may reduce the risk of certain cancers. Available fresh, frozen or as juice, blackcurrants can be quite tart but full of intense flavour. They make fabulous sorbets, smoothies and sauces, and are often a key ingredient in summer fruit combinations.

Blueberries
Dark purple in colour, blueberries have become very popular, and were probably among the first fruits to be labelled as a 'superfruit'. Their benefits came to the fore when studies revealed that they inhibited cancer cell development. These laboratory studies pointed to the blueberries' high phytonutrient content as a possible reason for these attributes. Their antioxidant activity is one of the highest ever measured in food. As well as anthocyanins, blueberries contain flavanols and tannins along with the particularly effective resveratrol, which is also found in grape skins and wine. Resveratrol is a naturally occurring anti-fungal compound produced by the plant to inhibit fungal growth on

the fruit. Other studies have pointed to beneficial effects in the battle against cognitive decline and Alzheimer's disease. The fruit is also thought to be good for lowering cholesterol and total blood fat levels. Its anti-inflammatory properties may help to reduce heart disease risk. However, it must be stressed that none of the benefits attributed to this superfood have yet been scientifically proven in human studies and further research is still needed.

Choose the berries that are plump and slightly firm, with a natural 'bloom'. Avoid any that are soft and dull-skinned, and wash and dry carefully to avoid bruising. Cultivated blueberries are larger than the wild variety, but both types are sweet enough to be eaten raw. They are good cooked in pies and muffins, can be used for jellies and jams, or made into a sauce to serve with nut or vegetable roasts. Unwashed blueberries will keep for up to a week in the bottom of the refrigerator.

Bilberries
These are from the same family as the blueberry and are sometimes referred to as the European blueberry. They are high in

anthocyanins, which are thought to help in the prevention of diseases such as heart disease, cancer and degenerative eye conditions. This has yet to be proven in humans but there is a tale of World War II pilots consuming bilberry jam specifically to improve their night vision when they went on missions. Fresh bilberries are uncommon, however, jams and conserves are more widely available.

Elderberries

Although elderberries are not commercially grown, when in season, they can easily be found growing in the wild. These large bushes are a common feature of many gardens and hedgerows, and both the flowers and berries have culinary uses. Pick the heads of the berries only when they are ripe, black and plump, as unripe berries contain a toxic alkaloid. Be sure to wash them thoroughly before use. Elderberry cordial and wine is made using the flower heads and not the berries, so it will not have the same benefits. The high levels of anthocyanins are specifically in the berries and are thought to help with the production of cell signalling compounds, which our body cells use to communicate with each other. This is a critical part of our immune response to pathogens such as bacteria, and so elderberries have been used for

Below: Anthocyanin-laden elderberries are ready to pick in the autumn.

Above: Nutrient-rich goji berries come in dried, juiced and powdered form.

many years to help with the relief of cold symptoms and for building up the immune system. As many parts of the bush have toxic compounds in them, it is advisable to cook the fruit.

Goji Berries

Also known as wolfberries, goji berries are grown in East Asia and have been used for centuries in Chinese Herbal Medicine as immune boosters and to aid circulation. Usually found in their dried form, they can be eaten like dried fruit, or they can be added to baked goods. They are also available as juices and in powdered form to add to drinks or make tea. Goji berries are good sources of many vitamins, minerals such as vitamin C, calcium and iron. They contain phytonutrients such as phytosterols, carotenoids (particularly zeaxanthin) and antioxidants, leading to many claims being made over their health benefits. These range from eyesight protection through to cardiovascular and anti-inflammatory effects as well as neuroprotective and anti-cancer properties. One must be aware that many scientific studies have been conducted to see if the claims can be proven, but to date

Above: Vitamin C-rich cranberries make a thirst-quenching juice.

they have not been conclusive. It is true, however, that the goji berry has an impressive array of nutrients, which mean its contribution to a healthy diet is substantial.

Cranberries

Mostly found frozen, dried or as a juice, the benefits of cranberries are varied. Native to North America, these little red berries have been used for many years to treat all sorts of conditions. Perhaps their best-known benefit is for urinary tract health. Compounds within the berries bind to bacteria and stop them from sticking to the wall of the urinary tract. How this actually helps during infection is yet to be fully understood. This anti-adhesion effect is thought to be why cranberry juice can also benefit oral health, as bacteria are prevented from sticking to gums and teeth.

Cranberries are also a rich source of polyphenol antioxidants and flavonoids, which have shown strong anti-cancer activity in laboratory studies; however, this effect is not proven in the human body. The dried fruits can be a little tart so try mixing them with other dried fruit or baking with them in place of raisins or sultanas. Avoid buying cranberry juices overloaded with added sugar.

GRAPES, MELONS, DATES AND FIGS

These fruits were some of the first ever to be cultivated and are therefore steeped in history. They are available in an immense variety of shapes, colours and sizes, and can be bought dried. As well as being a good source of nutrients, these fruits are high in soluble fibre.

Grapes

There are many varieties of grape, each with its own particular flavour and character, and most are grown for wine production. Eating varieties are less acidic, have a thinner skin than those used for wine-making and are more commonly seedless. Grapes range in colour from deep purple to pale red, and from bright green to almost white. Levels of anthocyanins (beneficial pigments) are higher in red grapes than in white, and this may be why more emphasis has been

Below: Black grapes have more anthocyanins than white grapes.

Above: White grapes contain heart-healthy nutrients.

placed on them; however, white grapes do still contain high levels of other flavonoids that have been shown to have beneficial effects, too.

The phytochemical content of grapes is mainly found in the skins, but grape seeds do yield tannins and, when crushed, an oil which is high in vitamin E and phytosterols. This oil can be used to cook with and is characterized by being very light, odourless and flavourless; because of

this it is often used as a carrier for other flavours. The darker the grape skin, the higher the phytochemical level. This high level of phytochemicals has led scientists to research the beneficial effects of grapes in areas such as heart health, cancer and Alzheimer's disease. Grapes contain resveratrol, a naturally occurring plant fungicide that affects how cancer cells grow and has anti-inflammatory

DRIED VINE FRUITS

Currants, sultanas (golden raisins) and raisins are the most popular dried fruits. Traditionally, these vine fruits are used for fruitcakes and breads, but currants and raisins are also good in savoury dishes. In Indian and North African cooking they are often used for their sweetness. It takes about 1.75–2.25kg/4–5lb fresh grapes to produce 450g/1lb sultanas, raisins or currants. Although high in natural sugars, which can damage teeth if eaten to excess between meals, dried fruit is a concentrated source of nutrients, including iron, calcium, potassium, phosphorus, vitamin C, beta-carotene and some of the B vitamins, and does contribute to your daily intake target of five fruit and vegetable portions.

Below: Dried raisins and sultanas all count towards your five-a-day.

properties. It is also being currently studied for its benefits to Alzheimer's patients and for treating specific cancers. Red and purple grape juices are also high in anthocyanins and polyphenols, and these have been shown in studies to reduce bad LDL cholesterol, increase good HDL cholesterol and reduce inflammation, all contributing to a reduction in heart disease risk. A particular variety, the Concord grape, has one of the highest antioxidant activity levels measured in foods, and products containing this juice are thought to be beneficial in the reduction of cholesterol levels.

Grapes are widely available and are easy to add to your family's diet. Whether as a small bunch in a lunch box with some cheese, or halved and sprinkled on a salad, grapes make a sweet, juicy addition to many savoury or sweet meal occasions.

When buying grapes, try to choose fairly firm, plump ones. The fruit should be evenly coloured and firmly attached to the stalk. Unwashed fruit may be stored in the refrigerator for up to five days.

Below: Red wine retains the heart-healthy nutrients found in grapes.

Above: The orange-fleshed cantaloupe melon is rich in beta-carotene.

Red Wine

Many of the phytochemicals found in the grape are stable enough to survive processing and fermentation during winemaking. The highly concentrated levels of phytochemicals that are found in red wine in particular has led to the coining of the phrase, 'The French Paradox'. This refers to the fact that the French population have a lower incidence of heart disease, even though their diet is relatively high in saturated fat. It is thought that, like red or purple grape juice, it is the high levels of resveratrol, polyphenols and antioxidants in red wine that contribute to this statistic. Most health professionals would not want to encourage over-consumption of alcohol and as is often the case, moderation is the key, so they often recommend one glass a day as suitable. Other commentators, however, have attributed the French paradox to the generally healthier diet and lifestyle of the French population. For example, their diet tends to include plenty of fish, olive oil and unprocessed foods, and they also generally have a less stressed approach to life.

Melons

This small family of fruits is split into two types; muskmelons and watermelons. Muskmelons include the varieties such as cantaloupe, charentais and honeydew, and usually have more flavour; watermelons, as their name suggests, have a far higher water content and so a less intense flavour. Watermelons

Below: Watermelon is rich in the anti-cancer nutrient lycopene.

Above: Figs are one of the richest non-dairy sources of calcium available.

are very low in calories because of their high water content, which is around 90 per cent. They contain less vitamin C and other nutrients than the fragrant, orange-fleshed varieties; however, watermelons are of particular interest because of their lycopene content, which is responsible for the lovely pinky red colour of the flesh. Lycopene has been shown to reduce the risk of prostate cancer, and a wedge of watermelon actually contains more lycopene than a cup of raw chopped tomato. Beta-cryptoxanthin is also found in

---

WATERMELON TIP
Because of its high water content, watermelon can be frozen to make healthy and refreshing ice pops – perfect for a hot summer day.
1 Slice the watermelon and remove the pips.
2 Cut each slice into long sections or fingers.
3 Pop the watermelon pieces in a plastic food container, seal and freeze overnight.

---

watermelon. It is a vitamin A precursor, that is a substance that the body can convert into vitamin A. The orange-fleshed varieties of melon contain useful levels of beta-carotene, also a vitamin A precursor, which is essential for a healthy immune system and normal growth and development.

When eaten on their own, melons pass quickly through the system. But, when consumed with other foods requiring a more complex digestive process, they may actually inhibit the absorption of nutrients.

Look for melons that feel heavy for their size and yield to gentle pressure at the stem end. Have a sniff of the skin and you should be able to smell the sweet flesh of the ripe melon.

Figs

The fig has been enjoyed for many thousands of years, and is thought to have been one of the first plants ever cultivated by humans. Figs are very high in fibre and are well known for their laxative properties. They are an excellent source of minerals such as calcium, magnesium, potassium and manganese. These delicate, thin-skinned fruits may be purple, brown or greenish-gold. They are very versatile: delicious raw, chopped up, added to natural yogurt and drizzled with honey for breakfast, served with soft cheese such as goat's cheese, and are a lovely complement for cured hams such as prosciutto or Parma ham. Figs can also be poached or baked lightly to make a delicious dessert. Choose unbruised, ripe fruits that yield to gentle pressure, and eat on the day of purchase. If they are not too ripe they can be kept in the refrigerator for a day or two. Figs are best eaten at room temperature, as chilling suppresses their juicy, sweet flavour. Dried figs are equally as nutritious and you only need to eat two to count as a portion of fruit. Dried figs, chopped or made into a paste, can be used in baking for a great moist addition to cakes, cookies and fruit loaves.

Above: High-fibre dates range in colour from yellow to dark brown.

Dates

Like figs, dates are one of the oldest cultivated fruits, possibly dating back as far as 50,000BC. Dates should be plump and glossy. Medjool dates from Egypt and California have a wrinkly skin, but most other varieties are smooth. They are high in soluble fibre and are very sweet. This sweetness gives them a very high glycemic index of 103, which is more than sugar at 100, so if you need an extremely fast burst of energy, eating a handful of dates will do the job. However, if you are looking to stabilize your sugar metabolism, you would be best to avoid them.

Fresh dates make a good natural sweetener for use in baking. You can purée the cooked fruit, then add this to muffin, cake or bread mixtures, or simply mix into natural yogurt to make a quick breakfast or dessert. Fresh dates can be stored in the refrigerator for up to a week. Dried dates can be kept in the store cupboard and added to cakes, cookies, scones and bread. You can also buy chopped dates and date paste, which can be used to replace some of the fat in fruit cake recipes.

TROPICAL FRUIT

This exotic collection of fruits ranges from the familiar bananas and pineapples to the more unusual papayas and guavas. The diversity in colour, shape and flavour is sure to excite the tastebuds as well as being pleasing to the eyes.

Papayas

Also known as pawpaw, these pear-shaped fruits come from South America. When ripe, the green skin turns a speckled yellow and the pulp is a glorious orange-pink colour. The ripe flesh is rich in vitamin C, folate and beta-cryptoxanthin, a type of carotenoid, which is a vitamin A precursor as well as an antioxidant. Green papaya is a good source of papain, an enzyme well known for its ability to tenderize meat and it is thought to possibly aid digestion. Papain preparations have also been used as a healing aid to treat cuts and burns by communities where papaya grows.

To eat, peel off the skin using a sharp knife or a vegetable peeler before enjoying the creamy flesh, which has a lovely perfumed aroma

Below: Vitamin-C and folate-rich, the ripe papaya tastes similar to a peach.

and sweet flavour. Ripe papaya is best eaten raw, while unripe green fruit can be used in cooking. The edible black seeds can be dried and ground. They taste like black pepper.

Mangoes

Across the family of tropical fruits, the mango accounts for approximately 50 per cent of all production, India being the largest contributor. The skin of these luscious, fragrant fruits can range in colour from green to yellow, orange or red. Their shape varies tremendously, too. An entirely green skin is a sign of an unripe fruit, although in Asia, these are often used in salads. Ripe fruit should yield to gentle pressure and, when cut, should reveal a juicy, orange flesh. This flesh has an impressive repertoire of nutrients and phytochemicals. Rich in vitamin C, vitamin A and vitamin E, its antioxidant credentials are improved further with beta-carotene, alpha-carotene and lutein, as well as an array of polyphenols. Mango also contains the essential minerals potassium and copper, and a wide range of amino acids. The

Below: Sweet mangoes have high levels of vitamins C, A and E.

skin is edible, and is a rich source of antioxidants, polyphenols and fibre. Served sliced or puréed, mango has a lovely creamy, juicy flavour which makes it an excellent base for smoothies, ice creams and sorbets.

PREPARING MANGO

Mangoes can be fiddly to prepare because they have a large, flat stone that is slightly off-centre. The method below produces cubed fruit. Alternatively, the mango can be peeled with a vegetable peeler and sliced around the central stone.

1 Hold the fruit with one hand and cut vertically down one side of the stone. Repeat on the opposite side. Cut away any remaining flesh around the stone.

2 Taking the two large slices, and using a sharp knife, cut the flesh into a criss-cross pattern down to the skin. Holding the mango skin-side down, press it inside out, and then cut the mango cubes away from the skin.

Above: A source of vitamin B6 and C, bananas make thick fruit smoothies.

Bananas

A concentrated bundle of energy, bananas are also full of valuable nutrients. The soft and creamy flesh can be blended into smooth, sweet drinks, mashed and mixed with yogurt, or the fruits can be baked and barbecued whole. Bananas also make an ideal weaning food for babies as they rarely cause an allergic reaction. Bananas are rich in dietary fibre and a variety of vitamins and minerals, especially potassium, which is important for the functioning of cells, nerves and muscles, and can relieve high blood pressure. They are also high in vitamin B6, vitamin C and manganese. Beware of banana chips, as they are actually deep fried slices of banana which are then coated in sugar or honey and so will be much higher in fat and calories. You can get dehydrated banana, but this is very leathery in texture and dark brown in colour. Choose fresh bananas that are not too green or bruised and ripen them at room temperature. Never store bananas in the refrigerator as they will quickly blacken, and always prepare immediately before serving, as they will discolour rapidly.

Kiwis

Also known as the Chinese gooseberry, a clue to its early origins, kiwi fruit was imported into New Zealand for commercialization in the early 20th century, where the population thought it tasted like a gooseberry. The name was changed to kiwi, as there were negative associations with China at the time. Kiwi fruit is extremely rich in vitamin C and the seeds have the omega-3, alpha-linoleic acid in them. It is high in fibre and this may be the reason for its usefulness as a gentle laxative. A Norwegian study has also indicated that kiwi fruit has a blood thinning effect, however, this was at quite a high level of consumption of two to three kiwi fruit a day for 28 days. The flesh also contains an enzyme called actinidin, which means it cannot be used in milk-based foods or jellies as the enzyme digests the protein. In addition, some people have a sensitivity to this compound which can cause itchiness and other allergic symptoms. The fabulous green colour of the kiwi makes it a welcome addition to fruit salads and fruit toppings, but it is just as delicious eaten on its own. Try cutting the top off, putting it in an egg cup and scooping out the flesh with a spoon, just like you would eat a boiled egg!

Below: Even the pips (seeds) in the kiwi fruit are full of essential nutrients.

BANANA TIP

A very ripe banana, past its best for eating, can be useful in another way. Ripe bananas give off a gas called ethylene, which can speed up ripening of other fruits such as pears, peaches or avocados. Simply place the under-ripe fruit into a bag or container along with the ripe banana and leave overnight at room temperature.

Acai Berries

The acai (pronounced A-sai-ee) berry is indigenous to South America and is commercially prepared as either a juice or a freeze-dried preparation of the skin and pulp. These berries contain a wide array of phytonutrients, which goes some way to explaining the vast number of conditions that they have traditionally been used to treat. Everything from heart health, elevated immune function and anti-cancer effects have been associated with acai berry consumption. Used for centuries by the South Americans, the berry has a high anthocyanin content and unusually contains fat that comprises the good mono-unsaturated and polyunsaturated fats. These, along with a moderate phytosterol content, are probably responsible for its healthy heart attributes by helping circulation, reducing blood clots, promoting good blood fats and preventing atherosclerosis. As if this wasn't enough, acai berries also have a considerably high level of antioxidants, which have been shown to reduce the proliferation of harmful cancer cells, but this has yet to be proven in humans. There have been claims about the berry's ability to promote rapid weight loss, but again there is little scientific proof of this. However, the berry's excellent nutrient profile, combined with a high fibre and omega-3 and -6 fat content, may contribute to a feeling of fullness.

The juice is popularly used for flavouring drinks and smoothies, and the fruit pulp is made into sorbets and yogurts.

Pomegranates

This ancient fruit originates from the Persian region and is now cultivated all over the Mediterranean. Underneath the leathery skin, the unusual bright red flesh-covered seeds make this a most interesting addition to any dish. Immersing the fruit in water makes it easier to remove the seeds from the outer pith and these are best eaten raw.

The juice of the pomegranate is very refreshing, not too sweet and is a good source of vitamin C. However, it is its antioxidant polyphenol content that is thought to be responsible for some of its more far-reaching health benefits. Mainly in the realm of heart health, these polyphenols can reduce risk factors such as atherosclerosis and blood pressure, as they are able to protect cells from oxidative stress. Similar to cranberry, pomegranate juice may also have anti-viral and anti-bacterial properties, especially in the mouth, and may protect against tooth decay.

Guavas

One of the more unusual tropical fruits, the pink/orange flesh of this fruit is juicy and sweet, and indeed

> **DRIED TROPICAL FRUIT TIP**
> It is possible to buy most of these delicious tropical fruits in a dried version. However, many of them are actually more akin to glacé (candied) fruits, as a lot of sugar is added in order to preserve the fruit. So look carefully at the ingredient list and bear in mind that sugar, glucose syrup, invert sugar syrup, glucose and sucrose are tell-tale signs of added sugar. There are dried products that do not contain these added sugars or syrups, so persevere, as it is worth it for the health of your teeth alone.

Below: Acai berry smoothie is rich in antioxidants and omega-3 and -6 fats.

Below: Pomegranate juice is full of heart-healthy polyphenols.

Below: Guava flesh and skin has a high vitamin-C content.

is often seen as an ingredient in smoothies and juices. The flesh provides a good range of vitamins and minerals and is an excellent source of vitamin C, vitamin A, folate and minerals such as potassium and copper. It has a high fibre content, which we all need to be eating more of to ensure good gut health. The high levels of vitamin C and A, along with polyphenols, contribute to a relatively high level of antioxidant activity; as usual, the darker the flesh, the higher the value will be.

A guava is ripe when the flesh yields easily if pressed gently. The whole of the guava fruit is edible and this even includes the skin, which has a high vitamin-C concentrate. The seeds can also be eaten although they can be quite hard.

Pineapples

Probably one of the most popular of the tropical fruits, the juicy sweet flesh of the pineapple is a versatile ingredient in sweet and savoury dishes as well as on its own. It is a good source of Vitamin C and manganese levels are also high. However, pineapple is unusual as it contains a unique enzyme called

Below: Sweet, juicy pineapple is delicious hot or cold.

bromelain, which has some interesting properties. Bromelain is a proteolytic enzyme, which means it can break down protein (similar to papain). It has traditional uses as a meat tenderizer where the juice can be used as a meat marinade. Bromelain has anti-inflammatory properties that have been particularly effective in the treatment of arthritis and sports injuries as well as sinusitis. However, it is doubtful that eating pineapple alone can provide enough bromelain to relieve these conditions, and so commercial preparations of bromelain are used medicinally. Canned pineapple is widely available, however, the heat processing that the fruit is subjected to destroys the bromelain content present.

Warmed pineapple tastes fabulous as the juiciness and flavours really develop and the sugars caramelize. Flash-grill (broil) or barbecue slices to heat the fruit without destroying the bromelain content.

The colour of the outer skin of a pineapple is not necessarily an indicator of ripeness. It is true that the skin does change colour as the fruit ripens, but it is also true that a green pineapple can be ripe to eat. A more accurate method is to simply sniff the base of the pineapple, and when it smells sweet and juicy it is ripe. If you are unable to smell anything, it is not yet ripe, if it smells fermented and like pear drops, it is over-ripe. You can speed up the ripening process by leaving the fruit in a warm sunny place; the heat will accelerate the breakdown of the starch contained within the flesh to form sugar and ripen the fruit.

PINEAPPLE TIP

When buying pineapples, look out for those that have fresh green spiky leaves, are heavy for their size, and are slightly soft to the touch. Always store ripe pineapples in the refrigerator.

PREPARING PINEAPPLE

1 Use a sharp knife to cut off the green leaves that form the crown and discard it.

2 With a sharp knife, remove the skin from the pineapple, cutting deeply enough to remove most of the 'eyes'.

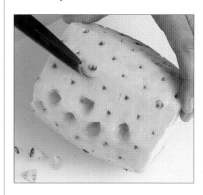

3 Use a small knife to carefully take out any 'eyes' that remain in the pineapple flesh.

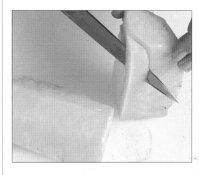

4 Cut the pineapple lengthwise into quarters and remove the core section from the centre of each piece. Chop the pineapple flesh or cut it into slices and use as needed.

Vegetables

Vegetables offer an infinite number of culinary possibilities for the cook. The choice is immense, and the growing demand for organic produce has meant that pesticide-free vegetables are now increasingly available. Vegetables are an essential component of a healthy diet and have countless nutritional benefits. They taste best and are most nutritious when freshly picked.

ROOTS AND TUBERS
Vegetables such as sweet potatoes, parsnips and carrots are comforting and nourishing, so it is not surprising that they should be popular in the winter. Their sweet, dense flesh provides sustained energy, valuable fibre, vitamins and minerals.

Parsnips
The parsnip is closely related to the carrot — not to the turnip as commonly believed. Parsnips are really just a paler, stronger-tasting version of the carrot. As they are not brightly coloured, they do not have the carotenes of the carrot, but they are still rich in vitamins C and K, folate, manganese and potassium. This vegetable has a particularly sweet, creamy flavour and is delicious roasted, puréed or steamed. Parsnips are best purchased after the first frost of the year as the cold converts their starches into sugar, enhancing their

Above: Carrots are an excellent source of vitamin A.

sweetness. Scrub before use and only peel if tough. Avoid large roots, which can be woody.

Carrots
The best carrots are not restricted to the cold winter months. Summer welcomes the slender, sweet new crop, often sold with their green, feathery tops. These are best removed after buying as they can rob the root of moisture and nutrients. Buy organic carrots if you can, because high pesticide residues have been found in non-organic ones. An added bonus is that organic carrots do not need peeling. A single carrot will supply enough vitamin A for an entire day's requirement. Some of this vitamin-A activity is derived from its precursors, alpha- and beta-carotene, which are also the antioxidants responsible for the bright orange colour. These carotenes are bound up in the structure of the carrot and are released through chopping and slicing; their availability can be improved further still by cooking in a little oil. The high levels of carotene are the reason why

Left: Creamy-tasting parsnips are rich in folate, manganese and potassium.

carrots are always cited as beneficial for healthy eyesight. Vitamin A is essential for vision, as it is a component of the visual pigments present in the retina of the eye. A deficiency of vitamin A leads to impaired vision and night blindness. The phytonutrient benefits of beta-carotene are being researched greatly in areas such as the prevention of lung cancer. There have been some conflicting results with respect to beta-carotene in isolation, and the most recent theories suggest that the best results are found when a combination of carotenoids is present. Carrots should be prepared

VIBRANT VEGETABLES
Always try to include a range of food colours in your diet and you'll ensure that you are consuming some fabulous phytonutrients. Beta-carotene is just one of the carotenoids found in green, yellow, orange and red vegetables (as well as fruit). Lycopene is another carotenoid which has a fabulous red-pink colour and is abundant in tomatoes, watermelon and pink guava. Most carotenoids are antioxidants, which slow down or prevent cell damage from free radical oxidation in the body. Vitamins C and E are other carotenoids, along with bioflavonoids. These help to enhance the immune system, which protects us against viral and bacterial infections and boosts the body's ability to fight cancer and heart disease. Chlorophyll, another antioxidant, is bright green and is therefore mainly found in green vegetables. Anthocyanin, a type of flavonoid, is responsible for the dark blues, reds and purples of beetroot, red onions and aubergines.

Above: Antioxidant- and mineral-rich beetroots act as liver cleansers.

just before use to preserve their valuable nutrients. They are delicious raw, steamed, roasted or puréed.

Beetroots (Beets)

Deep ruby-red in colour, beetroots add a vibrant hue and flavour to all sorts of dishes. They are often pickled in vinegar, but are better roasted, as this emphasizes their sweet, earthy flavour. Raw beetroot can be grated into salads or used to make relishes. If cooking the vegetable whole, wash carefully, taking care not to damage the skin, or the nutrients will leach out. Trim the stalks to 2.5cm/1in above the root. Small beetroots taste sweeter than larger ones.

Beetroot has long been considered medicinally beneficial and records show that the Romans often used it to treat fevers and as a laxative. It is an excellent liver cleanser, probably due to its high antioxidant levels. Beetroot is also a good source of folate and contains notable levels of vitamin C, manganese, potassium and magnesium. The beetroot's colour is due to the presence of betalain, a pigment compound similar to the anthocyanin family of compounds, not to be confused with betaine, which is also found in beetroot and is quite different. Betaine is able to protect blood vessels and bone collagen from damage due to excessive levels of homocysteine in the blood, and this may protect against vascular disease and bone weakness.

Celeriac

This knobbly root is closely related to celery, which explains its flavour – a cross between aniseed, celery and

Below: Celeriac is a diuretic and also contains vitamin C, calcium and iron.

parsley. Unlike most root vegetables, celeriac is not predominantly carbohydrate and therefore has approximately half the calories per 100g/3¾oz of potatoes. It must be peeled before use, and when grated and eaten raw in salads, celeriac has a crunchy texture. It can also be steamed, baked in gratins or combined with potatoes and mashed with butter or margarine and grainy mustard. Celeriac can also be used in soups and broths. Like celery, celeriac is a diuretic. It also a good source of vitamin C, vitamin K, calcium, iron, potassium and fibre.

Swedes (Rutabagas)

Globe-shaped swedes are part of the cruciferous vegetable family. Swedes contain many phytochemicals, such as the sulphurous compounds that are believed to have antioxidant and cancer-fighting properties. Like celeriac, they are a good source of vitamin A and vitamin C as well as potassium, and are lower in calories than the potato. Swede has pale orange flesh with a delicate sweet flavour. To prepare, trim off the thick peel, then treat it in the same way as other root vegetables. You can grate swede raw into salads; dice and cook it in casseroles and soups; or steam, then mash and serve it as an accompaniment to main dishes.

Below: Swede contains antioxidants that may help to prevent cancer.

Above: Highly nutritious baby turnips taste pleasantly peppery.

Turnips

This humble root vegetable has many health-giving qualities, as it is part of the important cruciferous vegetable family. Small turnips with their green tops intact are especially nutritious. Their crisp, ivory flesh enclosed in white, green and pink-tinged skin, has a pleasant, slightly peppery flavour, the intensity of which depends on their size and the time of harvesting. Small turnips can even be eaten raw. Alternatively, steam, bake or use in casseroles and soups. The green tops are rich in beta-carotene and vitamin C.

Potatoes

The sometimes-demonized potato has been blamed by many as being the reason for weight gain. However, potatoes are not in themselves fattening – it is the added ingredients such as butter or cheese and the cooking method that can often bump up the calories. Potatoes don't count as one of our 5-a-day because they are mainly carbohydrate, but they are an enormously important starchy food for many and are in fact the largest contributor to our vitamin-C intake. Their vitamins and minerals are stored in, or just below, the skin, so they're best eaten unpeeled. New potatoes and special salad potatoes need only be scrubbed. Steam rather than boil, and bake instead of frying to retain valuable nutrients and to keep fat levels down.

Potatoes provide plenty of sustained energy, as well as vitamin B_6, folate and potassium.

There are thousands of potato varieties, and many lend themselves to particular cooking methods. Small potatoes, such as Pink Fir Apple and Charlotte, and new potatoes, such as Jersey Royals, are best steamed. They have a waxy texture, which retains its shape after cooking, making them ideal for salads. Main crop potatoes, such as Estima and Maris Piper, are more suited to roasting, baking or mashing, and can be used to make chips. Discard any potatoes with green patches as these indicate the presence of toxic alkaloids called solanines.

Sweet Potatoes

A very distant relative of the potato, this bright yellow- or orange-fleshed vegetable is also known as a yam, especially in North America. However, it should not be confused with the white fleshed tuber, which is not as nutritious. Sweet potatoes can vary in shape, from short and stocky, like a traditional potato, through to long and tapered, and colour can range from yellow through to dark purple. The deeper the colour the more nutritious the vegetable will be. It is rich in the anti-oxidant beta-carotene as well as in fibre and vitamin B_6, and

Below: Vitamins and minerals are stored in or just under the potato skin.

SUPER VEGETABLE STOCK

Stock is easy to make at home and is a healthier option than shop-bought varieties, which are usually packed full of salt. Home-made stock can be stored in the refrigerator for up to four days. Alternatively, it can be prepared in large quantities and frozen. Use an ice cube tray so that you can defrost the amount that you need. Use this recipe when making the soups, stews, risottos, sauces and gravies featured in this book.

15ml/1 tbsp olive oil
1 sweet potato, chopped
1 carrot, chopped
1 onion, chopped
1 celery stick, chopped
2 garlic cloves, peeled
1 sprig of thyme
1 bay leaf
a few stalks of parsley
600ml/1 pint/2½ cups water
salt and freshly ground
    black pepper

1 Heat the oil in a large saucepan. Add the vegetables and cook, covered for 10 minutes or until softened, stirring occasionally. Stir in the garlic and herbs.

2 Pour the water into the pan and bring to the boil and simmer, partially covered for 40 minutes. Strain, season and use as required.

Above: Sweet potatoes are good source of fibre and beta-carotene.

contains reasonable amounts of iron, calcium and vitamin C, all of which make it a valuable starchy food. Due to its nutrient credentials and unlike the potato, the sweet potato does count as a 5-a-day portion. It can be prepared in a similar way to a potato, but its sweetness lends itself to many other uses such as in desserts – as pie fillings, for example. Never store sweet potatoes in a refrigerator as this causes the flesh to harden and will affect the flavour.

Jerusalem Artichokes
This small knobbly tuber has a sweet, nutty flavour and is related to the sunflower rather than arichoke family. Jerusalem artichokes contain surprisingly high levels of iron for a root vegetable and significant levels

Below: The Jerusalem artichoke is high in vitamin C and fibre.

Above: Vitamin C-rich, radishes also have diuretic properties.

of potassium. Peeling can be difficult, although scrubbing and trimming is usually sufficient. Store in the refrigerator for up to one week. Use in the same way as potatoes – they make good creamy soups.

Radishes
There are several types of this peppery-flavoured vegetable, which is a member of the cruciferous family. The round ruby red variety is most familiar; the longer, white-tipped type has a milder taste. Mooli or daikon radishes are white and very long; they can weigh up to several kilos or pounds. Radishes can be used to add flavour and a crunchy texture to salads and stir-fries. A renowned diuretic, radishes also contain vitamin C.

Horseradish
This pungent root is never eaten as a vegetable. It is usually grated and mixed with cream or oil and vinegar, and served as a culinary accompaniment. Its pungency is very effective in clearing blocked sinuses. Horseradish contains sinigrin, part of the glucosinolate family of phytochemicals, and this is an important compound being studied for its potential anti-carcinogenic properties. Seek out bright, firm, unwrinkled root vegetables, which do not have any soft patches. Whenever possible, choose organically grown produce, and purchase in small

Above: Wasabi (Japanese horseradish) is widely available in paste form.

quantities to ensure freshness. As with all root vegetables, store in a cool, dark place.

Wasabi
Also called the Japanese horseradish, wasabi is a cruciferous vegetable which contains the same glucosinolates as horseradish but in higher quantities. It is very effective at stimulating the nasal passages. Available either as a root or in paste form, wasabi is a traditional accompaniment to sushi and sashimi. Many commercial paste and powder preparations actually contain horseradish, not Japanese wasabi, and so won't be as strong. Read the ingredients list carefully looking for hon-wasabi, which is real Japanese wasabi.

Below: Horseradish contains potentially cancer-fighting sinigrin.

BRASSICAS

This large group of vegetables boasts an extraordinary number of health-giving properties. Brassicas are cruciferous vegetables and range from the crinkly-leafed Savoy cabbage to the small, walnut-sized Brussels sprout. These green, leafy vegetables include spinach, spring greens and kale.

Broccoli

This highly nutritious vegetable should be a regular part of everyone's diet. Two types are commonly available: purple-sprouting, which has fine, leafy stems and a delicate head, and calabrese, the more substantial variety with a tightly budded top and thick stalk. Raw broccoli is an excellent source of vitamin C but its levels decline as it is cooked, so keep cooking to a minimum.

Broccoli is also a good source of vitamin A and a range of B vitamins, most notably folate, which is essential if you are pregnant or planning a pregnancy. Minerals are abundant in this vegetable, including manganese, phosphorus, potassium, iron and calcium. As well as its enviable nutritional profile it also boasts some valuable phytonutrients. Broccoli contains sulphur compounds, which the body can convert into sulphoraphane, which helps with the

Above: Broccoli is one of the richest vegetable sources of folate.

elimination of carcinogens from the body, thus reducing cancer risk. Other sulphur compounds have anti-viral and anti-bacterial properties. These valuable compounds will leach into cooking water after about ten minutes so it is important not to boil broccoli for any longer. Better still, steam, microwave or stir-fry broccoli for a short time only.

Choose broccoli that has bright, compact florets. Yellowing florets, a limp, woody stalk and a pungent smell are an indication of overmaturity and an inferior nutrient profile. Trim stalks before cooking, although young stems can be eaten too, or serve raw in salads or with a dip.

Cauliflowers

The cream-coloured, compact florets should be encased in large, bright green leaves. There are other more brightly coloured varieties, such as orange and purple, but the cream version is the most common. This 'whiteness' by no means diminishes the nutritional profile of the cauliflower, as it is a rich source of vitamin C, vitamin K, folate, vitamin B_6, potassium and manganese, as well as being a good source of fibre. Its phytonutrient content is comparable to broccoli, including a wide range of the sulphur containing compounds that have been associated with reduced cancer risk. They work by stimulating the enzymes involved in the elimination of carcinogens.

Below: Cauliflower is a good source of cancer-fighting phytochemicals.

PREPARING BROCCOLI

Trim the stalks from the broccoli and divide it into florets. The stems of young broccoli can be sliced and eaten, too.

To get the most nutrients from a cauliflower, eat it raw in salad, bake with a cheese sauce or steam lightly. Cauliflower has a mild flavour and is delicious tossed in vinaigrette dressing or combined with tomatoes and spices in a curry. Overcooked cauliflower is unpleasant, has a sulphurous taste and is reduced to mush. Avoid cauliflowers that have black spots or yellowing leaves.

Cabbages

This is another member of the cruciferous family of vegetables. Many people have had a bad experience with cabbage, usually due to overcooking the vegetable to a sloppy mush that smells sulphurous and unpleasant. Cabbage is best eaten raw, or cooked until only just tender. There are several different varieties: Savoy cabbage has substantial, crinkly leaves with a stronger flavour and is perfect for stuffing or gently steaming; firm white and red cabbages can be shredded and used raw in salads or for pickling, while pak choi (bok choy) is best cooked in stir-fries or eaten with noodles.

All varieties are excellent sources of fibre, vitamins A, C, B6 and K as well as folate, manganese, potassium and magnesium. Cabbage is also an

Below: Eat vitamin-rich cabbage raw or steamed for optimum nutrition.

MIXED CABBAGE STIR-FRY

Stir-frying is a quick method of cooking that retains much of the vitamins and minerals that are lost during boiling; it remains crisp and keeps its vivid colour.

15ml/1 tbsp groundnut or sunflower oil
1 large garlic clove, chopped
2.5cm/1in piece fresh root ginger, chopped
450g/1lb/5 cups mixed cabbage leaves, such as Savoy, white, curly kale or pak choi (bok choy), finely shredded
10ml/2 tsp soy sauce
5ml/1 tsp runny honey
5ml/1 tsp toasted sesame oil (optional)
15ml/1 tbsp sesame seeds, toasted

1 Heat the oil in a wok or large, deep frying pan, then sauté the garlic and ginger for about 30 seconds. Add the cabbage and stir-fry for 3–5 minutes until tender, tossing frequently.

2 Stir in the soy sauce, honey and sesame oil and cook gently for 1 minute. Sprinkle with sesame seeds and serve.

excellent source of beneficial sulphur-containing compounds, which, as well as showing effective anti-cancer activity, can also reduce inflammation by tempering the activity of white blood cells. This may explain why cabbage leaves have long been used to treat inflammation such as engorged, sore breasts in women who are breast-feeding. Raw or juiced cabbage is particularly potent and also has antiviral and antibacterial qualities. Again, the quicker you can cook cabbage the better, as this will retain the most nutrients. When choosing, you should select cabbages that have a heavy heart, and Chinese cabbages should be compact and heavy for their size with bright, undamaged leaves.

Above: Brussels sprouts contain plant sterols – natural cholesterol reducers.

Brussels Sprouts

These are basically miniature cabbages that grow on a long, tough stalk, and they have a strong nutty flavour. They have one of the highest concentrations of sulphurous compounds including those that the body converts to sinigrin, which in research has been shown to destroy pre-cancerous cells and may be able to prevent colon cancer. They are excellent sources of fibre, vitamins A, B_6, C and K, as well as folate, potassium and manganese. Their folate content may also contribute to their anti-cancer properties, as it is involved in DNA repair in the cell.

PREPARING BRUSSELS SPROUTS

1 Peel off any outer damaged leaves from the Brussels sprouts.

2 Before cooking, cut a cross in the base of each sprout, so that they cook quickly and evenly.

Brussels sprouts also contain plant sterols, which are natural cholesterol reducers.The best are the small ones with tightly packed leaves – avoid any that are very large or turning yellow or brown. Sprouts are sweeter when picked after the first frost. They are best cooked very lightly, so either steam or, better still, stir-fry to keep their green colour and crisp texture, as well as to retain their vitamins and minerals.

GREEN LEAFY VEGETABLES

For years we have been told to eat up our greens and now we are beginning to learn why. Research into their health benefits has indicated that eating dark green leafy vegetables, such as spinach, spring greens, chard and kale, on a regular basis may protect us against certain forms of cancer. These quite fragile, green, leafy vegetables do not keep well – up to 2 or 3 days at most. Eat soon after purchase to enjoy them at their best. Look for brightly coloured, undamaged leaves that show no signs of yellowing or wilting.

Spinach

This dark, green leaf is a superb source of cancer-fighting antioxidants and has an impressive vitamin and mineral content. It contains about four times more beta-carotene than broccoli and also has very high levels of lutein and zeathanthin, which are both found in the lens of the human eye. This has provoked some interesting studies of which results suggest that people who had high intakes of lutein and zeathanthin largely from spinach were up to 50 per cent less likely to have cataract problems. Spinach does contain good levels of iron, but it is in a form that is not easily absorbed – spinach contains oxalic acid, which inhibits the absorption of iron and binds any calcium present. However, eating spinach with a vitamin C-rich food will increase absorption. Spinach contains an immense amount of

Above: Iron-rich spinach tastes great in salads or added to hot dishes.

vitamin K, essential for the blood clotting process and is a good source of vitamins A, C and E, folate and riboflavin. Other minerals present in good amounts are magnesium, potassium and manganese. Nutritionally, it is most beneficial when eaten raw in a salad or steamed lightly, as boiling can halve the levels of folate.

Watercress

The hot, peppery flavour of watercress complements milder tasting leaves and is classically combined with fresh orange or fruit. Watercress is a member of the

Below: The lutein and beta-carotene in watercress are strong anti-oxidants.

cruciferous family and shares its cancer-fighting properties due to the presence of sulphur containing compounds. Watercress also contains beta-carotene and lutein, both of which are powerful antioxidants. It is rich in vitamins A, C and K, and also in calcium, manganese and potassium. Watercress can be used fresh in salads, where it adds a peppery zing, or it can be used to make soups or sauces. It does not keep well and is best refrigerated and eaten within two days of purchase.

Spring Greens (Collard Greens) and Curly Kale

These leafy, dark green young cabbage leaves are all very similar and are all the same cultivar. Rich in vitamin A, C and especially K, spring greens have an excellent beta-carotene, lutein and zeathanthin profile, giving them exceptional antioxidant credentials. They are also rich in a wide range of sulphur-containing compounds including indole-3-carbinol, which in studies has been shown to affect oestrogen metabolism and may therefore be of use in preventing reproductive organ cancers, although this is unproven in humans. The availability of these compounds can be increased by chopping up spring greens, releasing the sulphur compounds and essential enzymes required to convert them into their active forms. Keeping cooking times to a minimum will also help to retain all of the nutrients, stir-frying or steaming being the best options.

Swiss Chard

Part of the same family as beetroot, this vegetable is grown for its highly nutritious leaves. Similar to spinach, Swiss chard has a more robust, slightly bitter flavour and is best eaten when the leaves are young and tender. Swiss chard is very rich in antioxidants such as vitamins A and C and a variety of flavonoids. It contains one of the highest

Above: Kale contains chlorophyll, iron, calcium and vitamins A and C.

Above: Swiss chard is one of the best sources of vitamin K.

concentrations of vitamin K known. The leaves are quite fragile and do not keep well, so should be eaten as soon as possible, either in a salad or wilted in a steamer. The stalks are edible, but need to be cooked for longer.

IMPORTANCE OF PHYTOCHEMICALS

Cruciferous vegetables, such as broccoli, cabbages, kohlrabi, radishes, cauliflowers, Brussels sprouts, watercress, turnips, kale, pak choi (bok choy), spring greens (collards), chard, and spinach, are particularly valuable because of the cocktail of phytochemicals that are found in them. This mix includes the antioxidant vitamins A, C and E, folate, fibre, phytosterols, glucosinolates, isothiocyanates, phenols, chlorophyll, lignans, flavonoids and minerals such as selenium and potassium. This heady mix of powerful compounds may be particularly effective in eliminating carcinogens from the body before they can go on to damage DNA. Additionally, some cell-signalling pathways could be altered to prevent cells becoming cancerous. While no specific intake guidelines for this family of vegetables exist, some tests have suggested that adults should aim for at least five portions of cruciferous vegetables a week to get the most potential benefit.

Below: Choose smaller pak choi varieties with firm stalks and leaves.

Below: Both the leaves and the bulb of the kohlrabi can be eaten.

VEGETABLE FRUITS

In cultivation and use, tomatoes, avocados and peppers are all vegetables, but botanically they are actually classified as fruit. Part of the nightshade family, it is only relatively recently that they have become appreciated for their health-giving qualities.

Aubergines (Eggplants)

A good source of folate and fibre, aubergines also contain moderate amounts of potassium, manganese and B vitamins. The dark-purple, glossy-skinned aubergine is the most familiar variety and, as its skin colour suggests, is a rich source of anthocyanins. These flavonoid compounds are potent antioxidants.

The small, ivory-white, egg-shaped variety is probably responsible for its name 'eggplant' in the USA, and is not such a rich source of anthocyanins. There is also the bright-green pea aubergine that is used in Asian cooking, and a pale-purple Chinese aubergine. Known in the Middle East as 'poor man's caviar', aubergines give substance and flavour to spicy casseroles and

Below: The dark-purple skin of the aubergine is rich in antioxidants.

tomato-based bakes, and are delicious roasted, griddled and puréed for garlic-laden dips. It is not essential to salt aubergines to remove any bitterness; however, this method prevents the absorption of excessive amounts of oil during frying. When buying, look for small to medium aubergines, which have sweet, tender flesh. Large specimens with a shrivelled skin are over-mature and are likely to be bitter and tough. Aubergines can be stored in the refrigerator for up to two weeks.

Tomatoes

These widely consumed fruits vary in colour, shape and size according to which of the vast number of varieties are available. All share one major benefit; they are an excellent source of lycopene. This powerful antioxidant has been the subject of much research in the field of cancer prevention, especially that of the prostate. Studies of populations suggest that diets high in lycopene have up to a 20 per cent lower risk of prostate cancer. About 80 per cent of our lycopene intake comes from tomatoes, so it is an important source. You should note, however, that the cooking and processing of tomatoes increases the bioavailability of lycopene, with tomato paste being the most concentrated source. So, in this case it is better to make tomato soup or sauces to maximize your lycopene intake. However, raw tomatoes are still important as they are good sources of other vitamins and minerals, as well as fibre.

Plum tomatoes are perfect for cooking as they have a rich flavour and a high proportion of flesh to seeds – but they must be used when fully ripe. Too often, shop-bought tomatoes are bland and tasteless because they have been picked too young. Vine-ripened and cherry tomatoes are sweet and juicy and are good in salads or uncooked sauces. Large beefsteak tomatoes have a good flavour and are also excellent

PEELING AND SEEDING TOMATOES

Tomato seeds can give sauces a bitter flavour. Removing them and the tomato skins will also give a smoother end result.

1 Immerse the tomatoes in boiling water and leave for about 30 seconds – the base of each tomato can be slashed to make peeling easier.

2 Lift the tomatoes out of the bowl using a slotted spoon, rinse in cold water to cool slightly, and peel off the skin.

3 Halve the tomatoes, then scoop out the seeds and remove the hard core. Dice or roughly chop the flesh according to the recipe.

Above: Juicy vine-ripened tomatoes are rich in vitamin C.

Above: Capsaicin, found in chillies, may have anti-cancerous properties.

for salads. Sun-dried tomatoes add a rich intensity to sauces, soups and stews. Look for deep-red fruit with a firm, yielding flesh. To improve the flavour of a slightly hard tomato, leave it to ripen fully at room temperature. Avoid refrigeration because this stops the ripening process and adversely affects the taste and texture of the tomato.

Chillies
Native to the Americas, this member of the capsicum family now forms an important part of many cuisines, including Indian, Thai, Mexican, South American and African. Chillies do actually contain more vitamin C weight for weight than an orange, although we only eat them sparingly because of the heat factor. They also contain notable concentrations of vitamins K and B6, as well as folate, potassium and manganese. Chillies contain beta-carotene and a unique family of phytochemicals called capsaicinoids, of which capsaicin is the heat-producing compound predominantly found in the seeds and flesh. These stimulate the release of endorphins by binding to heat

sensors on the tongue. This sends a message to the brain causing an increased heart rate and the release of endorphins, which are the body's natural painkiller. Chillies stimulate the body and improve circulation, but if eaten to excess can irritate the stomach. Capsaicin may also have other effects such as the ability to kill cancer cells, reduce LDL cholesterol, alleviate stomach ulcer symptoms and contribute toward pain relief. There are more than 200 different types of chilli, ranging from the long, narrow Anaheim to the lantern-shaped and incredibly hot Habañero.

Red chillies are not necessarily hotter than green ones – but they will probably have ripened for longer in the sun. The heat-inducing capsaicin is found mainly in the seeds, white membranes and, to a lesser extent, in the flesh. Chillies range in potency from the mild and flavourful to the blisteringly hot. Dried chillies tend to be hotter than fresh. Smaller chillies, such as bird's eye chillies, contain proportionately more seeds and membrane, which makes them more potent than larger ones. Always handle chillies with care and

wash your hands afterwards as they can irritate the skin and eyes. Choose unwrinkled, bright, firm chillies and store in the refrigerator.

Olives
Originating from the Mediterranean region, along with olive oil, these little gems have become iconic because of the phenomenon of the 'Mediterranean Diet'. High levels of monounsaturated fat and low levels of saturated fat, among other factors, have contributed to a low incidence of heart disease in the region. Olives are also high in the fat-soluble vitamins A and E, as well as in copper and calcium.

Traditionally, black olives were those that were allowed to ripen fully on the tree; they are sometimes known as natural black olives. It is far more common, however, to see olives that have been processed to become black. These black olives start as green olives from the tree which are then held in tanks to oxidize and turn black; they are then allowed to cure in a salted brine before packing. Green olives are picked before they have a chance to

Below: Olives offer a good source of vitamins A and E, calcium and copper.

PEELING PEPPERS

1 Roast the peppers under a hot grill for 12–15 minutes, turning regularly until the skin is charred and blistered. Alternatively, you can place on a baking tray and roast in an oven preheated to 200°C/400°F/Gas 6 for 20–30 minutes, until the skin is blackened and blistered.

2 Put the peppers in a plastic bag and leave until cool – the steam will encourage the skin to peel away easily.

3 Peel off the skin, then slice in half. Remove the core and scrape out any remaining seeds. Slice or chop according to the recipe.

Above: Sweet and vibrant, peppers are rich in vitamin C.

ripen and are then cured and packed. This serves two purposes; it reduces the bitterness of a freshly picked olive and it enables the olive to be preserved. Green olives tend to taste slightly bitter and have a stronger flavour than black olives. Chop up olives and add to your favourite salad or pizza topping.

Peppers
Like chillies, sweet or bell peppers are also members of the capsicum family. They range in colour from green through to orange, yellow, red and even purple. Green peppers are fully developed but not completely ripe, which can make them difficult to digest. They have refreshing, juicy flesh with a crisp texture. Other colours of peppers are more mature, have sweeter flesh, and are more digestible than less ripe green peppers. Peppers are very high in vitamin C and the carotenoids b-cryptoxanthin and lycopene, all of which exhibit powerful antioxidant activity. They are also a good source of fibre, vitamins A, K and B6, as well as potassium and manganese. Roasting or chargrilling peppers will enhance their sweetness. They can also be stuffed, sliced into salads or steamed. Always try to choose

peppers that are firm and glossy with an unblemished skin, and store in the refrigerator for up to a week.

Avocados
Although avocados have a high fat content, most of the fat is monounsaturated; these healthier fats are thought to help lower bad LDL cholesterol levels in the body without affecting the good HDL fats. Avocados also contain valuable amounts of a host of other vitamins and minerals; in particular, they are high in vitamins C, K and B6, niacin, folate and pantothenic acid as well as notable amounts of potassium, copper, magnesium and manganese. Avocados have one of the highest fibre contents of all of the fruits, and this comprises both insoluble and soluble fibre, with one avocado providing around 9g/1¼oz of fibre. Those on diets high in fibre have consistently been shown to have lower coronary heart disease risk and lower incidence of Type II diabetes.

Once cut, avocados should be brushed with lemon or lime juice to prevent discoloration. Usually eaten raw, avocado halves can be dressed with vinaigrette, or filled with sour cream or hummus and sprinkled with cayenne pepper. In Mexico, where

Below: Fibre-rich avocados are good for reducing coronary risk.

they grow in abundance, guacamole is the most common dish, but avocados are also used in soups and stews.

MUSHROOMS

Thanks to their rich earthiness, mushrooms add substance and flavour to all sorts of dishes. There are more than 2,000 edible varieties but only a tiny proportion are readily available. These fall into three camps: common cultivated mushrooms, like the button (white); wild varieties that are now cultivated, such as the shiitake; and the truly wild types that have escaped cultivation, such as the morel. Mushrooms have been used for their medicinal properties over thousands of years and have been the subject of great scientific breakthroughs, such as the discovery of modern-day statin drugs for the treatment of high cholesterol. Much revered in ancient times, mushrooms have been researched extensively and it is thought to be their complex polysaccharide structure, containing beta-glucan, that is partly responsible for their properties.

The shiitake and the maitake mushrooms have the highest concentrations of beta-glucan compounds, and this sets them apart from the hundreds of other mushrooms available. In general, mushrooms are a low-fat, high-fibre food that are integral to many of our favourite dishes.

Button (White), Cap and Flat Mushrooms

The most common cultivated variety of mushrooms, these are actually the same variety in various stages of maturity. The button mushroom is the youngest and has a tight, white button-like cap. It has a mild flavour and can be eaten raw in salads. Cap mushrooms are slightly more mature and larger in size, while the flat mushroom is the largest and has dark, open gills. Flat mushrooms are the most flavoursome and are good

grilled or baked on their own, or stuffed. Researchers at Pennsylvania State University in the USA found these common white mushrooms to have extremely high levels of the powerful antioxidant, L-Ergothioneine.

Shiitake Mushrooms

The shiitake mushroom is native to China and has been grown in that region for hundreds of years. Used widely in Chinese, Japanese and Korean cuisine since ancient times, it has been recognized that they are not just a nutritious food source but also that they possess medicinal properties.

The shiitake mushroom contains high concentrations of lentinan, a particular type of beta-glucan. This highly purified extract, has been researched extensively as an anti-tumour agent and for its immune regulation properties. It is an approved cancer drug in Japan, but has yet to reach this status elsewhere.

These mushrooms have also been shown to reduce cholesterol levels and are thought to have anti-viral and anti-fungal properties. They are available fresh or dried, the latter being more intense in flavour and a more concentrated source of the active agents. The dried mushrooms

Below: Shiitake mushrooms have particularly high levels of beta-glucan.

need to be re-hydrated by soaking before they are added to dishes such as soups, risottos or pies. These mushrooms have a strong, almost meaty, flavour.

Maitake Mushrooms

The maitake mushroom grows in a wonderful cluster formation and is often found at the base of an oak tree. It can grow to as large as 60cm/24in in diameter. As well as being rich in many minerals, maitake mushrooms contain the beta-glucan compounds thought to be an immune system stimulator, and which recent research has shown to have anti-cancer properties. Often available only in supplement form, if you are lucky enough to come across the maitake mushroom, use it like any other mushroom, lightly steamed or added to soups or risottos.

THE ONION FAMILY

Onions and garlic are highly prized as two of the oldest remedies known to man. What is more, these versatile vegetables are indispensable in cooking. The wide variety of onions can be enjoyed raw or cooked and, with garlic, add flavour to a huge range of savoury dishes.

Garlic

For centuries, this wonder food has been the focus of much attention, and is praised for its medicinal powers, which range from curing toothache to warding off evil demons. Garlic is rich in organosulphur compounds, which are converted to allicin when the clove is chopped or crushed. These compounds have been shown to decrease the production of cholesterol by liver cells, have anti-inflammatory effects, prevent clogging and act as vasodilators of arteries. All of these properties will contribute in some way to a reduced risk of cardiovascular disease. Allicin can also affect the metabolism of carcinogens in the body by inhibiting certain enzymes that activate these

Below: Garlic's properties are thought to be due to the potent compound allicin.

Above: Chopping onions releases the beneficial compounds.

carcinogens, thus potentially reducing cancer risk. Population studies suggest that a high intake of garlic may protect against gastric and colorectal cancer. Allicin also shows some antibacterial and antifungal qualities. This is most effective, however, when used raw in an ointment preparation rather than taken internally. The flavour of garlic is milder when whole or sliced; crushing or chopping releases the oils, making the flavour stronger. Slow-cooking also tames the pungency of garlic, although it still affects the breath. Most garlic is semi-dried to prolong its shelf life, yet the cloves should still be moist and juicy. Young garlic, which is available in early summer, has a long green stem and soft white bulb. It has a fresher flavour than semi-dried garlic, but can be used in the same ways. Pungency varies, but the general rule when buying garlic is the smaller the bulb, the more potent the flavour. If stored in a cool, dry place and not in the refrigerator, garlic will keep for up to about eight weeks. If the air is

damp, garlic will sprout, and if it is too warm the cloves will eventually turn to grey powder.

Onions and Shallots

Every cuisine in the world includes onions in one form or another and, along with garlic, they are often the first thing that is cooked. Like garlic, chopping the onion releases the organosulphur compounds that are then converted to allicin. Onions are an essential flavouring, offering a range of taste sensations, from the sweet and juicy red onion and powerfully pungent white onion to the light and fresh spring onion (scallion).

GARLIC TIP

In order to loosen the skin and make the garlic cloves far easier to peel, push down on each clove with the heel of a large chopping knife.

Above: Red onions are packed with antioxidant flavonols.

Pearl onions and shallots are the babies of the family. Tiny pearl onions are generally pickled, while shallots are stronger in flavour and are good roasted with their skins on, when they develop a caramel sweetness. Spring onions are the only onions that are generally eaten raw, as they are not so strong as the other varieties. Yellow onions are the most common and are highly versatile. As well as being a good source of allicin, all onions, and red onions in particular, are a good source of flavonols such as quercetin, a very active compound which has been shown to have anti-inflammatory and anti-cancer properties as well as being a potent antioxidant. Shallots show the highest antioxidant activity and the greatest concentrations of these flavonoid polyphenols. When buying, choose onions that have dry, papery skins and are heavy for their size. They will keep for 1–2 months when stored in a cool, dark place.

Leeks

Like onions and garlic, leeks have a very long history. They grow in all sorts of climates and are known to have been eaten and enjoyed by the ancient Egyptians, Greeks and Romans. Leeks are very versatile, having their own distinct, subtle

Above: Shallots have particularly potent quercetin levels.

flavour. They are less pungent than onions but are still therapeutically beneficial. Leeks have the same active constituents as onions, but in smaller amounts. They are an excellent source of vitamins A, C and K as well as vitamin B6 and folate. They contain considerable amounts of iron and manganese as well as calcium, magnesium and copper. Much of the nutritional goodness is in the green part of the leek, so don't discard too

Below: Avoid leeks without their roots, as they deteriorate more rapidly.

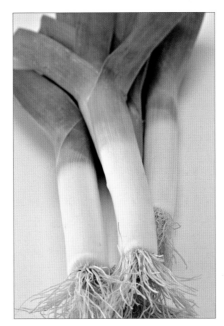

much of this. Excellent in soups and casseroles, leeks can also be used as a pie filling or in flans, or simply steamed and served hot with a light, creamy sauce, or cooled slightly and dressed with a vinaigrette. They are also delicious sliced or shredded and then stir-fried with garlic and ginger. Choose firm leeks with bright green leaves. Leeks will keep for up to a week in the refrigerator.

CLEANING LEEKS

Leeks need meticulous cleaning to remove any grit and earth that may hide between the layers of leaves. The following method should ensure that the very last tiny piece of grit will be washed away.

1 Trim off the root, and then trim the top of the green part and discard. Remove any tough or damaged outer leaves.

2 Slash the top green part of the leek into quarters then rinse the leek well under cold running water, separating the layers to remove any hidden dirt. Slice or leave whole, depending on the recipe.

PUMPKINS AND SQUASHES

Widely available in the USA, Africa, Australia and the Caribbean, pumpkins and squashes come in a tremendous range of shapes, colours and sizes. Squashes are broadly divided into summer and winter types, of which butternut squash and pumpkins are winter examples.

Butternut Squashes

Also known as a type of winter squash, the bright orange flesh of the butternut makes a very attractive addition to many dishes. Its natural sweetness makes this a popular vegetable with children, and it can spruce up plain mashed potato with its flavour and colour. As its bright orange colour might suggest, it is packed full of carotenoids, which not only have vitamin A activity but are also strong antioxidants. As with carrots, the availability of these carotenoids is increased by chopping or mashing, which releases them from the cell structure; a little oil also helps. Butternut squash also contains a decent amount of vitamin C and

Above: Roasted butternut squash is a rich source of vitamin A.

manganese, which have antioxidant properties, and also potassium, which plays an important role in muscle function, especially that of the heart. Roasting butternut squash will concentrate its flavour and sweetness. Alternatively, simply boiling it and adding to a soup mix will give added body and creaminess without the need to add any cream.

Pumpkins

Another winter variety, pumpkins are rich in all of the carotenoids, which include alpha-carotene, beta-carotene and beta-cryptoxanthin, all powerful antioxidants. Pumpkins also contain lutein and zeathanthin; both of these carotenoids are found in the eye and may protect against age-related macular degeneration. They are native to the USA, where they are synonymous with Thanksgiving and Halloween celebrations. Small pumpkins have sweeter, less fibrous flesh than the large ones. Deep orange in colour, pumpkin can be used in both sweet and savoury dishes, such as pies, soup, casseroles and souffles. When cooking pumpkin, you should avoid boiling it as it can become waterlogged and soggy.

ROASTING SQUASH

1 Preheat the oven to 200°C/400°F/Gas 6. Cut the squash in half, scoop out the seeds and place the squash cut-side down on an oiled baking tray.

2 Bake for 30 minutes or until the flesh is soft. Serve in the skin, or remove the flesh and mash with butter.

PEELING PUMPKIN

1 Cut the pumpkin in half using a large sharp knife and scoop out the seeds and fibrous parts with a spoon.

2 Cut the pumpkin into large chunks, then cut off the skin using a sharp knife.

SHOOT VEGETABLES

This collection of vegetables refers to those plants that bear perennial fruit above the ground, ranging from the aristocratic asparagus to the flower bud-like globe artichoke. A wide range of flavours, shapes and textures are represented, but all are highly prized vegetables with some interesting credentials.

Fennel

Florence fennel is closely related to the herb of the same name. The short, fat bulbs have a similar texture to celery and are topped with edible feathery fronds. Fennel has a mild aniseed flavour, most potent when eaten raw. Cooking tempers the flavour, giving it a delicious sweetness. Fennel contains a complex compound called anethole, thought to be responsible for its carminative effects, having a soothing effect on the intestines and reducing flatulence. There are also studies suggesting that anethole may have beneficial effects on inflammation in the body. When using fennel raw, slice it thinly or chop roughly and add to salads. Alternatively, slice or cut into wedges and steam, or brush with olive oil and roast or cook on a griddle. Choose bulbs that are firm, without splitting or bruising. Fennel is at its best when fresh and should be eaten as soon after harvesting as possible as its flavour diminishes with time. It can, however, be stored in the refrigerator for a few days.

Globe Artichokes

These vegetables have a particularly good mineral profile, which includes very high levels of magnesium, manganese, copper and potassium. They are also a good source of folate and vitamin K. The fibre content of the artichoke is one of the highest in the vegetable family, and this has many health benefits, such as maintaining good cholesterol levels and general bowel health.

Cooked artichoke leaves are eaten with the fingers by dipping them into garlic butter or a vinaigrette dressing then drawing each leaf through the teeth and eating the fleshy part. The leaves of the globe artichoke contain an interesting substance called cynarin. This bitter-tasting compound has

long had associations with liver health and is reputed to assist regeneration of liver cells; it is also involved in cholesterol metabolism. Cynarin also stimulates gallbladder activity and has been shown to have benefits in digestive health. To date, however, clinical trials are inconclusive on the areas of liver function and cholesterol metabolism.

Asparagus

Highly valued since Roman times, asparagus has been cultivated commercially since the 17th century. There are two main types: white asparagus is picked just before it sprouts above the surface of the soil, while green-tipped asparagus is cut above the ground and develops its colour when it comes into contact with sunlight. It takes three years to grow a crop from seed, which may account for its expense.

Asparagus is very rich in vitamin K and the B-vitamins, folate and riboflavin. Folate is essential for the healthy development of the foetus as it has a crucial role in DNA synthesis. To prepare asparagus for use, first scrape the lower half of the stalk with a vegetable peeler and then trim off the woody end. Asparagus tastes best when it is lightly steamed or boiled. If boiling, try to use a tall pan so that the tips are out of the water and are able to steam-cook while the tougher stalks can cook in the boiling water.

Below: Fennel provides an excellent source of the essential vitamin K.

Below: Lightly steam asparagus to retain all the valuable minerals.

PREPARING GLOBE ARTICHOKES

1 Hold the top of the artichoke firmly and, using a sharp knife, remove the stalk and trim the base so that the artichoke is able to sit flat.

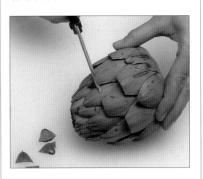

2 Using a sharp knife or scissors, trim off and discard the tops of the leaves and cut off the pointed top.

3 Cook the artichokes in a pan of lightly salted boiling water for 35–45 minutes, until a leaf can be pulled out easily. Carefully drain the artichokes upside down.

4 Pull out the central leaves, then scoop out the hairy choke with a teaspoon and discard.

Herbs

Herbs have been highly prized by natural practitioners for centuries because, in spite of their low nutritional value, they do contain phytonutrients that possess numerous reputed healing qualities. Many of these phytonutrients are found in the essential oils of these plants, which give them their amazing pungency. These essential oils have high levels of antioxidant activity and many herbs feature in the top 50 foods with the highest ORAC scores. In cooking, herbs can make a significant difference to the flavour and aroma of a dish and they have the ability to enliven the simplest of meals. Fresh herbs can be easily grown at home in the garden, or in a pot or window box.

Basil

One of the most popular fresh herbs in the kitchen, sweet basil is used extensively in Mediterranean cooking and complements tomato dishes especially well. The essential oils

Below: Herbs can be grown easily in flowerbeds, pots and window boxes.

Above: The beta-carophyllene in basil has anti-inflammatory qualities.

of sweet basil leaf are of particular interest as they are potent antioxidants and therefore of interest in cancer research. There have also been studies into a compound called beta-carophyllene (BCP), a natural anti-inflammatory compound also found in oregano but better known as a constituent of cannabis. The BCP in basil and oregano has

PESTO

Freshly made pesto, spooned over warm pasta or spread over bread and topped with a round of goat's cheese, makes a perfect quick supper. It is usually made with basil, but other herbs, such as rocket, coriander (cilantro) or parsley, can be substituted. The pine nuts can also be replaced with walnuts, cashew nuts or pistachio nuts.

50g/2oz/1 cup fresh basil leaves
2 garlic cloves, crushed
40g/1½oz/½ cups pine nuts
120ml/4fl oz/½ cup olive oil, plus extra for drizzling
60ml/4 tbsp freshly grated Parmesan cheese
salt and black pepper

1 Place the basil, garlic and pine nuts in a food processor or blender and process until finely chopped.

2 Gradually add the olive oil and then the Parmesan, and blend to a coarse purée. Season to taste. Spoon into a lidded jar, then pour over the extra olive oil to cover. Use immediately, or store in the refrigerator for 3–4 days.

BOUQUET GARNI

Combining the wonderful aromatic flavours of some fabulous herbs, a bouquet garni is essentially a bunch of mixed herbs, tied together with string or wrapped in muslin (cheesecloth). Classic combinations include sage, thyme and bay but its not unusual to see parsley, tarragon or rosemary with a few black peppercorns. Many savoury recipes call for a base sauce or stock to be flavoured with a bouquet garni. The bouquet is boiled with the base liquid and is then removed prior to serving the dish.

Right: A bouquet garni can contain whatever herbs you have to hand.

anti-inflammatory properties without the mood-altering effects of cannabis. Basil leaves do bruise easily and begin to turn brown, so always use immediately and towards the end of the cooking time.

Below: Fresh lemon balm has anti-viral and anti-bacterial properties.

Lemon Balm

The fragrant broad leaves of this herb are particularly good for making a refreshing herbal tea and go well with mint. Lemon balm can be added to any sweet or savoury dish that uses lemon juice or mint and can also be used to replace citrus peel in recipes. Lemon balm is said to have some calming and mild sedative attributes and could be beneficial for those suffering from stress or nervous exhaustion. It also has antibacterial and antiviral qualities, due to its eugenol and tannin content. It is also claimed to make a good mosquito repellent when rubbed on the skin.

Mint

The most familiar types are spearmint and peppermint, but there are other distinctly flavoured varieties, such as apple, lemon and pineapple mint, which are worth looking out for, and make a refreshing drink when infused in boiling water. Mint contains the essential oil menthol, which is a traditional cure for nausea and indigestion, and is also effective as a decongestant when you are suffering from a cold, especially if you inhale the steam of the mint infusion.

FREEZING HERBS

This is an excellent method of preserving fresh delicate herbs such as basil, chives, dill, tarragon, coriander (cilantro) and parsley. The herbs will lose their fresh appearance and texture when frozen, but are still suitable for use in cooking. They will keep for up to 3 months in the freezer.

• Half-fill ice-cube trays with chopped herbs and top up with water. Freeze, then place the cubes in freezer-bags. The frozen cubes can be added to soups, stews and stocks, and heated until they melt.

• Place whole sprigs or leaves, or chopped herbs in freezer bags, expel any air and tightly seal.

• Freeze herb sprigs or leaves on trays. When the herbs are frozen, transfer them carefully to freezer-bags, expel any air, seal tightly and return to the freezer.

• Pack chopped fresh herbs in plastic pots and freeze. Sprinkle into soups and stews straight from the freezer.

Mint is used as a flavouring in a wide variety of dishes, from stuffings to fruit salads, and as a sauce with lamb dishes. Mint is a vital ingredient in the Middle Eastern salad tabbouleh, and is also mixed with natural yogurt to make raita, a soothing accompaniment to hot curries.

Oregano

The oregano plant is actually a species of mint and is a perennial herb used extensively in Mediterranean cooking. It goes well with vegetable and meat dishes and even spicy foods. Its potential benefits to health are linked to its high phenolic and flavonoid content, which is associated with very high antioxidant activity. Try adding the chopped fresh or dried leaves to tomato dishes, sprinkle on grilled meats or mix with olive oil and lemon juice for a classic Greek dressing.

DRYING HERBS

Bay, rosemary, sage, thyme and marjoram all dry well. However, other more delicate herbs, such as basil, coriander (cilantro) and parsley, are better used fresh. Pick herbs before they flower, preferably on a sunny morning after the dew has dried. Avoid washing them – instead, brush with a pastry brush or wipe with a dry cloth. Tie the herbs in bunches and hang them upside down in a warm, dark place. The leaves should be dry and crisp after a week. Leave the herbs in bundles or strip the leaves from the stems and store in airtight jars.

Above: Mint's essential oil, menthol, is used to treat nausea and indigestion.

Rosemary

Wonderfully aromatic, rosemary is traditionally used in Mediterranean cuisine, particularly for meat dishes, but it can also add a smoky flavour to hearty bean and vegetable dishes. Rosemary has a high antioxidant content from a wide range of compounds such as rosmarinic acid and carnosic acid. This antioxidant activity may protect the body

Below: Oregano is a good source of antioxidant phenols and flavonoids.

USING DRIED HERBS

Although fresh herbs have the best flavour and appearance, dried herbs can be a convenient and useful alternative, especially in the winter months when some fresh herbs are not available.
• A few herbs such as basil, dill, mint and parsley do not dry well, losing most of their flavour.
• Oregano, thyme, marjoram and bay retain their flavour when dried and are useful substitutes for the fresh herbs.
• Dried herbs have a more concentrated flavour than fresh, so much less is required – usually a third to half as much as fresh.
• When using dried herbs in cooking, always allow sufficient time for them to rehydrate and become soft.
• Dried herbs do little for uncooked dishes, but are useful for flavouring marinades, soups and slow-cooked stews.
• When buying dried herbs, they should look bright, not faded and, because light spoils their flavour and shortens shelf-life, store in sealed, airtight jars in a cool, dark place.

from free-radical damage, and the antioxidant carnosic acid has been studied for its potential benefits in the field of brain degenerative diseases; results suggest that it may offer some protection to the brain. This could go some way to explaining its traditional reputation for memory improvement. Add sprigs of rosemary to roasted dishes or strip the small green leaves from the woody stem if adding to stocks or soups.

Sage

Native to the Mediterranean region, the silver-grey or purple leaves of this herb have a potent aroma and only a small amount is needed. Sage is commonly added to meat dishes but, if used discreetly, it is delicious with beans, cheese, lentils and in stuffing. Interestingly, the Latin name for sage, *Salvia*, actually means 'healing', and gives us an insight into the heritage of this herb as a far-reaching healing aid throughout the centuries. In more recent times, sage has been found to contain a variety of phytosterols and flavonoids, which may explain its potential use in relieving menopausal symptoms. Other areas which have been studied more extensively are its effects on reducing excessive sweating and saliva production, as a tonic for the stomach and possibly as an aid to Alzheimer's disease management. The essential oils in sage also have antibiotic and antiviral properties, and are good for external use on insect bites and skin infections.

Thyme

This robustly flavoured aromatic herb tastes good in tomato-based recipes, and also goes well with roasted vegetables, lentils and beans. It is also an essential ingredient in a bouquet garni. Thyme contains a compound called thymol, which is

a powerful antiseptic and is widely used in mouthwash formulations. Tinctures of thyme have traditionally been used to relieve symptoms of sore throats and coughs. Because thyme is more of a robust woody herb, it delivers its flavour far better if added at the beginning of the cooking process.

Below: Thyme's antiseptic properties make it an excellent mouthwash.

Above: Sage contains beneficial phytosterols and flavonoids.

MAKING HERBAL INFUSIONS
Infusions, or tisanes, are made by steeping fresh herbs in boiling water. Infusions can be used as a refreshing healthy drink or a medicinal gargle. Peppermint tea drunk after a meal is an excellent remedy for indigestion.

To make peppermint tea: pour boiling water over fresh peppermint leaves. Cover and leave to stand for about ten minutes, then strain the liquid into a cup and drink.

Below: Rosemary contains the active antioxidant rosmarinic acid.

Sea vegetables

Western societies have only relatively recently acknowledged the amazing variety and remarkable benefits of sea vegetables, which have been an essential part of the Asian diet for centuries. Versatile sea vegetables can be used as the main component of a dish, to add texture and substance, or as a seasoning. They are usually sold in dried form and will keep for months.

Health Benefits

The health benefits of sea vegetables have been recognized for centuries, and range from improving the lustre of hair and clarity of the skin to reducing blood cholesterol levels. Sea vegetables have significant amounts of the major minerals, such as iron, calcium, magnesium, potassium and phosphorus, and useful amounts of trace elements, such as selenium and zinc. They are particularly high in the essential mineral, iodine, which helps efficient thyroid function. They are also rich in the antioxidant beta-carotene and contain some of the B-complex vitamins.

The rich mineral content of sea vegetables benefits the nervous system, helping to reduce stress. It also boosts the immune system, aiding metabolism. Research shows that alginic acid found in some seaweeds, notably kombu, arame, hijiki and wakame, binds with heavy metals, such as cadmium, lead, mercury and radium, in our intestines and can help to eliminate them.

Above: A bowl of nori flakes.

Nori

This useful sea vegetable has a delicate texture and mild flavour. It is sold in thin purple-black sheets, which turn translucent green when toasted or cooked. It is one of the few sea vegetables that does not require soaking. In Japanese cooking, nori sheets are used to wrap small parcels of vinegared rice and vegetables that are eaten as sushi. Toasted nori is used as a garnish.

Laver

A relation of nori which grows outside Japan, laver is commonly found around the shores of Britain. It is used in traditional regional cooking – particularly in Wales, Scotland and Ireland. It is cooked to a thick purée, which can be spread on toast or mixed with oatmeal to make laverbread. It can also be added to sauces and stuffings. Available ready-cooked in cans, laver has a particularly high concentration of vitamins and minerals.

Wakame

This sea vegetable is often confused with its relative, kombu, because it looks very similar until it is soaked, when it changes colour from brown to a delicate green. Wakame has a mild flavour and is one of the most versatile of sea vegetables. Soak briefly, then use it in salads and soups, or toast, crumble and use it as a condiment. It is rich in calcium and vitamins B and C.

Kombu

Also known as kelp, kombu is a brown sea vegetable that is most commonly sold in dried strips. It has a strong flavour and is used in slowly cooked dishes, soups and stocks. Kombu is an essential ingredient in the Japanese stock, dashi. It is richer in iodine than other sea vegetables, and is also rich in calcium and potassium, as well as iron.

Arame

Sold in black strips, arame has a mild, slightly sweet flavour. It needs to be soaked before using in stir-fries or salads, but if using in moist or slow-cooked dishes, such as noodles and soups, it can be added straight from the packet. Arame is rich in iodine, calcium and iron, and is used to treat high blood pressure.

Carrageen

This fern-like seaweed, also known as Irish moss, is found along the Atlantic coasts of North America

---

TOASTING NORI
Nori sheets can be toasted over an electric or gas hob until they turn crisp. Be careful not to scorch the nori – or your fingers.

1 Hold a sheet of nori with a pair of tongs about 5cm/2in above an electric hot plate or gas hob for about 1 minute, moving it around so it toasts evenly and turns bright green and crisp.

2 Leave the nori sheet to cool, then crumble. Add to stir-fries or sprinkle over salads and soups.

and Europe. Like agar-agar, it has gelling properties but produces a softer set, making it useful for jellies and mousses and as a thickener in soups and stews. Carrageen is used for treating colds and bronchial ailments as well as digestive disorders.

Hijiki
This sea vegetable looks similar to arame but is thicker and has a slightly stronger flavour. Once soaked, hijiki can be sautéed or added to soups and salads, but it needs longer cooking than most sea vegetables. Hijiki expands greatly during soaking, so only a small amount is needed. It is particularly rich in calcium and iron.

Dulse
A purple-red sea vegetable, dulse has flat fronds, which taste spicy when cooked. It needs to be soaked until it turns soft before adding to salads, noodle dishes, soups and vegetable dishes. It can also be toasted and crumbled for a nourishing garnish.

Below: Hijiki strands will expand greatly on soaking, so use sparingly.

Dulse is rich in several important minerals, including iodine, potassium, phosphorus, manganese and iron.

Agar-agar
The vegetarian equivalent to the animal-derived gelatine, agar-agar has a neutral taste and can be used as a setting agent in both sweet and savoury dishes. It can be bought as flakes or strands, both of which need to be dissolved in water before use. Agar-agar is more effective than gelatine, so only a small amount is needed. It is also said to be an effective laxative.

Chlorella
A type of green algae and a relative of seaweed, chlorella is a good source of protein, vitamins and minerals. In the past it was considered to be the answer to the world's food production problems in the light of rapidly growing populations, but large-scale production difficulties meant that it did not fulfil its potential.

Chlorella has many reputed health benefits and has been clinically proven to help reduce blood pressure and blood cholesterol levels. There is also evidence that it could help our immune response and speed up wound-healing. Available as tablets or in powdered form, chlorella can be added to food and drink or taken as a supplement.

Below: Marsh samphire has a salty flavour that complements fish dishes.

Above: Agar-agar is an extremely good source of dietary fibre.

Spirulina
Also an algae, spirulina has an unusually high concentration of protein. It contains a good range of essential fatty acids including the omega-3 family, and has an excellent vitamin and mineral profile. It is high in antioxidants such as beta-carotene. Its reputed health benefits include lowering cholesterol and improving heart health. Its concentrated nutritional profile could make it a useful food source for the future.

Available in tablet and powdered form, spirulina has a slightly bitter flavour. The powder can be added to drinks such as juices or smoothies.

Marsh Samphire
Also known as sea asparagus, this unusual plant grows in coastal areas on the mud flats of salt marshes. It resembles a mini cactus, and its succulent flesh is a delicacy. Growing close to the sea, it shares many of the same characteristics as seaweed, being a rich source of chlorophyll and minerals, such as iodine and zinc.

Marsh samphire is not readily available in shops but can be found at your local fishmonger. Alternatively, at the start of the season in June, visit the sea shore at low tide and forage for yourself. Steam it gently and serve with a little butter or olive oil. Eat by pulling off the juicy flesh with your teeth.

Sprouted seeds, grains and pulses

Sprouts are quite remarkable in terms of nutritional content. Once the seed (or pulse or grain) has germinated, the nutritional value rises dramatically. There are almost 30 per cent more B vitamins and 60 per cent more vitamin C in the sprout than in the original seed, pulse or grain. The sprouting process also results in an increase in the activity of many enzymes that remain dormant in the dry seed, grain or pulse. This enhanced enzyme activity is then able to break down carbohydrates, proteins and fats into simpler compounds and new compounds, making them more bio-available to us. Supermarkets and health food shops sell a variety of sprouts. If you can, choose fresh, crisp sprouts with the seed or bean still attached. Avoid any that are brown, slimy or musty-looking, or have a strange odour. Sprouts are best eaten on the day they are bought but, if fresh, they will keep,

WARNING
People with weakened immune systems, as well as the very old and the very young, should not eat raw sprouts.

TIPS ON SPROUTING
• Use whole seeds and beans, as split ones will not germinate.
• Regular rinsing with fresh water and draining is essential when sprouting, to prevent the beans from turning rancid and mouldy.
• Cover the sprouting jar with muslin (cheesecloth) to allow air to circulate and water in and out.
• After two or three days, the jar can be placed in sunlight to encourage the green pigment chlorophyll and increase the sprout's magnesium and fibre content.

wrapped in a plastic bag, in the refrigerator for 2–3 days. Rinse thoroughly and pat dry before use. It is also easy to grow them at home – all you need is a jar, some muslin (cheesecloth) and an elastic band.

Mung Beansprouts
These widely available beansprouts, are popular in Asian cooking, where they are used in soups, salads and stir-fries. They are fairly large and crunchy, with a delicate flavour. If you are cooking them, do so for only a few seconds to retain some crunch.

Lentil Sprouts
These sprouts have a slightly spicy, peppery flavour and thin, white shoots. You should use only whole lentils, as split ones will not sprout.

Alfalfa Sprouts
These tiny, wispy white bean-sprouts have a mild, nutty flavour and are related to the pea.

Above: Alfalfa beansprouts are an excellent source of phytoestrogens.

Above: Mung beansprouts

Above: Lentil sprouts

SPROUTING SEEDS, PULSES AND GRAINS

Larger pulses, such as chickpeas, take longer to sprout than small beans, but they are all easy to grow and are usually ready to eat in three or four days. Store sprouts in a covered container in the refrigerator for 2–3 days.

1 Wash 45ml/3 tbsp seeds, pulses or grains thoroughly in water, then place in a large jar. Fill the jar with lukewarm water, cover with a piece of muslin (cheesecloth) and fasten securely with an elastic band. Leave in a warm place to stand overnight.

2 The next day, pour off the water through the muslin and refill the jar with water. Shake gently, then turn the jar upside down and drain thoroughly. Leave the jar on its side in a warm place, away from direct sunlight.

3 Rinse thoroughly three times a day until they reach the desired size. Remove the contents from the jar, rinse and remove any ungerminated beans.

These sprouts contain phytoestrogens, which have a mild oestrogen-mimicking effect in the body, and have been used to alleviate menopausal symptoms. They are best eaten raw to retain their crunchiness.

Aduki Beansprouts

These fine wispy sprouts have a sweet nutty taste and are particularly good in salads and stir-fries.

Wheat Berry Sprouts

Sprouts grown from wheat berries have a crunchy texture and sweet flavour and are excellent in breads. If they are left to grow, the sprouts will become wheatgrass, a powerful detoxifier that is usually made into a juice.

Chickpea Sprouts

These sprouts are grown from chickpeas and have a wonderful nutty flavour. These sprouts will add a crunchy texture and some substance to your salads and side dishes.

Above: Aduki beansprouts

Above: Wheat berry sprouts

Right: Chickpea sprouts

HOW TO USE BEANSPROUTS

• Sprouted pulses and beans have a denser, more fibrous texture, while sprouts grown from seeds are lighter. Try using a mixture of all three to vary the tastes and textures.

• Sprouted grains are good in breads, adding a pleasant, crunchy texture. Knead them in after the first rising, before shaping the loaf.

• Mung beansprouts are often used in Asian cooking, particularly in stir-fries, and require very little cooking.

• Chickpea and lentil sprouts are ideal for use in casseroles and bakes.

• Alfalfa sprouts are good as part of a sandwich filling as well as in salads. They are not suited to cooking.

CEREAL GRAINS

Grains have been cultivated throughout the world for hundreds of years. The seeds of cereal grasses are packed with concentrated goodness and are an important source of complex starchy carbohydrates, protein, vitamins and minerals. When eaten as wholegrains they offer us the most health benefits, and many health organizations have guidelines that recommend we eat at least three portions of wholegrain a day. The most popular types of grain, such as wheat, rice, oats, barley and corn or maize, come in various forms, from wholegrains to flours. Inexpensive and readily available, these grains are incredibly versatile and should form a major part of our diet.

Wheat

The largest and most important grain crop in the world, wheat has been cultivated since 7,000BC. The wheat kernel comprises three parts: bran, germ and endosperm. Wheat bran is the outer husk, while wheat germ is the nutritious seed from which the plant grows. The endosperm, the inner part of the kernel, is full of starch and protein and forms the basis of wheat flour. In addition to flour, wheat comes in various other forms. Wheat is most nutritious when it is unprocessed and in its

Below: Wheat berries

wholegrain form. Indeed, when milled into white flour, wheat loses a staggering 80 percent of its nutrients.

Wheat Berries

These are whole wheat grains with the husks removed, and they can be bought in health food shops. Wheat berries may be used to add a sweet, nutty flavour and chewy texture to breads, soups and stews, or can be combined with rice or other grains. Wheat berries must be soaked overnight, then cooked in boiling salted water until tender. If they are left to germinate, the berries sprout into wheatgrass, possibly a powerful detoxifier and cleanser (see opposite).

Wheat Flakes

Steamed and softened, berries that have been rolled and pressed are known as wheat flakes or rolled wheat. They are best used on their own or mixed with other flaked grains in porridge (oatmeal), as a base for muesli, or to add nutrients and substance to breads and cakes.

Wheat Bran

The outer husk of the wheat kernel, wheat bran is a by-product of white flour production. It is very high in insoluble dietary fibre, which makes it an effective laxative as it increases bulk. It is an extremely good source of almost all of the B vitamins – only B_{12} is absent – as well as all the essential minerals except sodium, although the phytate content of the bran can reduce the absorption of

COOKING WHEAT BERRIES
Wheat berries make a delicious addition to salads, and they can also be used to add texture to breads and stews.

1 Place the wheat berries in a bowl and cover with cold water. Soak overnight, then rinse thoroughly and drain.

2 Place the wheat berries in a pan with water. Bring to the boil, then cover and simmer for 1–2 hours until tender, replenishing with water when necessary.

calcium and iron quite considerably. Wheat bran makes a healthy addition to bread doughs and breakfast cereals, as well as cakes and biscuits.

Below: Wheat flakes

WHEATGRASS – A NATURAL HEALER?

Grown from the whole wheat grain, wheatgrass has been recognized for centuries for its general healing qualities. However, this has not been proven within the realms of modern scientific research. It does contain a good range of B vitamins, including vitamin B12, which is unusual in a non-meat source, as well as vitamins A, E, and a little vitamin C. Its vibrant green colour comes from chlorophyll, which may be able to bind with harmful toxins and help the liver to eliminate them, although this has not been scientifically proven. Once it is juiced, wheatgrass must be consumed within 15 minutes, preferably on an empty stomach.

Wheat Germ

The nutritious heart of the whole wheat berry, wheat germ is an excellent source of protein, the B vitamins (except B12) and all of the essential minerals. It is higher in

Below: Bulgur wheat

fat than wheat bran, but this is a polyunsaturated oil, and includes both omega-3 and omega-6 essential fatty acids. Wheat germ is one of the richest sources of phytosterols, which can reduce the total cholesterol and the 'bad' LDL cholesterol in the blood, and therefore reduce heart disease risk. It is is used in much the same way as wheat bran and is available toasted or untoasted, lending a nutty flavour to breakfast cereals and porridge. Because of its higher oil content, store wheat germ in an airtight container in the refrigerator, as it can become rancid if kept at room temperature.

Cracked Wheat

This is made from crushed wheat berries and retains all the nutrients of wholewheat. Often confused with bulgur wheat, cracked wheat can be used in the same way as wheat berries (although it cooks in less time), or as an alternative to rice and other grains. When cooked, it has a slightly sticky texture and pleasant crunchiness. Serve it as an accompaniment, or use it in salads.

Bulgur Wheat

Unlike cracked wheat, this grain is made from cooked wheat berries, which have the bran removed, and are then dried and crushed. This light, nutty grain is simply soaked in water for 20 minutes, then drained – some manufacturers specify cold water but boiling water produces a softer grain. It can also be cooked in boiling water until tender. Bulgur wheat is the main ingredient in the Middle Eastern salad tabbouleh, where it is mixed with chopped parsley, mint, tomato, cucumber and onion, and dressed with lemon juice and olive oil.

Above: Wheat germ

COELIAC DISEASE

Distinct from a wheat allergy or intolerance, this auto-immune condition is triggered by an intolerance to gluten, a type of protein found in many cereals, but most commonly wheat. It damages the lining of the small intestine and reduces the ability to absorb nutrients properly. Unfortunately, the intolerance is permanent and the only way to manage the disease is to avoid gluten-containing foods totally. It often manifests itself with abdominal discomfort or weight loss, but less severe symptoms are very common too and it can go undiagnosed for some time.

This diagnosis is critical and diagnostic blood tests can be used to indicate intolerance, however, a trained practitioner should carry this out, as false positives are common.

Sometimes a more invasive gut biopsy may also be necessary. A gluten-free diet is a major undertaking as such a great proportion of the western diet includes wheat. Expert advice from your GP or dietician should be sought, to ensure that no further dietary issues arise when excluding such a large food group from the diet.

RICE

Throughout Asia, a meal is considered incomplete without rice. It is a staple food for over half the world's population, and almost every culture has its own repertoire of rice dishes, ranging from risottos to pilaffs. What is more, this valuable food provides a good source of vitamins and minerals, as well as a steady supply of energy.

Choosing the Rice

Which rice you choose will depend largely on the meal you intend to cook. Basmati, with its wonderful fragrance and flavour, is for many the only rice to serve with an Indian meal. For a Chinese, Thai or Indonesian meal, Thai fragrant rice, with its pleasant aroma and slightly sticky texture (important if you intend to use chopsticks) is excellent, while the versatile American long grain rice is great for stir-fries, pilaffs, jambalayas and gumbos.

There are a few instances where only a specific type of rice will do – risottos, for example, can only be made successfully with risotto rice – but in general, providing you know a little about the qualities of the rice, there are no hard and fast rules. Although tradition demands rice puddings be made with a short grain rice, there's no reason why you

Below: Brown rice contains more nutrients than refined white rice.

Above: Rice is the main energy source for much of the world's population.

shouldn't use long grain. Basmati and even Thai fragrant rice make delicious puddings, too.

Storing Rice

Raw (uncooked) rice can be kept in a cool, dark place for up to three years in the unopened packet or in an airtight container. It should be kept perfectly dry; if the moisture content creeps up, the rice will turn mouldy. If the rice is very old, it may need more water or longer cooking. Check the packet for 'best before' dates. Cooked rice can be stored for up to 24 hours if cooled, covered and kept in the refrigerator. You can also freeze the cooled rice; reheat it in a covered casserole in the oven or thaw it and use it for fried rice or in a salad. The rice should should be piping hot all the way through and should only be reheated once.

Brown Rice

Brown rice is a valuable source of complex carbohydrates and insoluble fibre. This whole rice form contains a higher proportion of B vitamins than white rice because the bran and germ have not been removed. The starch in brown rice is absorbed more slowly, keeping blood sugar levels on an even keel and making it an important food for diabetics. Brown rice and rice bran contain a

COOKING LONG GRAIN RICE

There are many methods and opinions on how to cook rice. The absorption method is one of the simplest and retains valuable nutrients, which would otherwise be lost in cooking water that is drained away.

Different types of rice have different absorption powers, but the general rule of thumb for long grain rice is to use double the quantity of water to rice. For the following method, use 1 cup of brown long grain rice to 2 cups of water. 200g/7oz /1 cup long grain rice is sufficient for about four people as a side dish.

1 Rinse the rice in a sieve (strainer) under cold, running water. Place in a heavy-based pan and add the measured cold water. Bring to the boil, uncovered, then reduce the heat and stir the rice. Add salt, to taste, if you wish.

2 Cover the pan with a tight-fitting lid. Simmer for 25–35 minutes, without removing the lid, until the water is absorbed and the rice tender. Remove from the heat and leave covered for 5 minutes before serving.

polyphenol called g-oryzanol which has been extracted and studied for its effects in people with high cholesterol levels; the results show that it could reduce total cholesterol in these people. It is also gluten free.

Basmati Rice

This is a slender, long-grain rice, which is grown in the foothills of the Himalayas. It is aged for a year after harvest, giving it a characteristic light, fluffy texture and aromatic flavour. Its name means 'fragrant'. Both white and brown types of basmati rice are available. Choose brown basmati as it contains more nutrients, and has a slightly nuttier flavour than the

Below: The short grains of risotto rice are also good for rice puddings.

white variety. Widely used in Indian cooking, basmati rice has a cooling effect on spicy curries. It is also excellent for rice salads, when you want very light, fluffy separate grains.

Risotto Rice

For risotto, you need to use a special, fat, short grain rice. Arborio rice is the most widely sold variety. When cooked, most rice absorbs around three times its weight in water. Risotto rice can absorb nearly five times its weight, which results in a creamy grain that retains a slight bite.

Camargue Red Rice

This rice comes from the Camargue region in France and has a distinctive chewy texture and a nutty flavour. It is an unmilled brown rice that is unusually hard, which, although it takes about an hour to cook, retains its shape. The red-coloured outer bran is a good source of fibre, vitamins and minerals. This type of rice also has a lower glycaemic index than white rice, so it is good for slow-release energy. Cooking intensifies its red colour, making it a good addition to salads and stuffing.

Wild Rice

This is not a true rice but an aquatic grass grown in North America. It has dramatic, long, slender brown-black

Below: High in fibre, wild rice actually belongs to the grass family.

grains that have a nutty flavour and chewy texture. It takes longer to cook than most types of rice – 35–60 minutes, depending on whether you prefer it chewy or tender – but you can reduce the cooking time by soaking it in water overnight. Wild rice is extremely nutritious. It contains all eight essential amino acids and is particularly rich in lysine. It is a good source of fibre, is low in calories and gluten-free. Use in stuffings, or mix with other rices in pilaffs and salads.

Rice Bran

Like wheat and oat bran, rice bran comes from the husk of the grain kernel. It is high soluble dietary fibre and useful for adding texture and substance to bread, cakes and biscuits (cookies) as well as to stews.

QUICK WAYS TO FLAVOUR RICE

• Cook brown rice in vegetable stock with sliced dried apricots. Sauté an onion in a little oil and add ground cumin, coriander and fresh chopped chilli, then mix in the cooked rice.

• Add raisins and toasted almonds to saffron-infused rice.

OTHER GRAINS

Wheat, oats and rice are undoubtedly the most widely used grains, yet there are others such as barley, quinoa and buckwheat, that should not be ignored, because they provide variety in our diet, are packed with nutrients and are classed as wholegrains. The versatile grain comes in many forms, from whole grains to flour, which are used widely in baking, breakfast cereals and many cooked dishes.

Oats

Available in many different guises, all oats have slightly different attributes and uses. One thing is true of all variations: the oat is a very healthy food to eat for a number of reasons. As well as being high in B vitamins, vitamin A and iron and manganese, it is one of the only foods to have satisfied both the American FDA and the UK FSA rules on health claims for its benefits for heart health. This is because oats contain a high level of soluble fibre, one of which is called beta-glucan, which has been proven to reduce overall cholesterol levels. One other effect of the soluble fibre is to slow down the energy release from the oat food and therefore make you feel fuller for longer. Most oat-based foods will have a good glycaemic index.

Below: Pearl barley makes a tasty low-glycaemic index risotto.

Rolled Oats and Oatmeal

This popular product is made when whole oats are hulled, removing the hard outer husk leaving a whole kernel. This can then either be cut into smaller pieces or rolled under heavy rollers. This process retains the bran and the germ and all of the nutrients associated with them. Quick-cooking rolled oats have been pre-cooked in water and then dried, deactivating the enzymes that can cause oats to go rancid. It is a popular grain in northern Europe, particularly Scotland, where they are commonly turned into porridge, oatcakes and pancakes. Medium oatmeal is best in cakes and breads, while fine is ideal in pancakes, as well as for fruit- and milk-based drinks.

Oat Bran

If the oat groat is rolled several times, the oat bran eventually separates out, leaving oat flour. High in soluble fibre and retaining a good proportion of the vitamins and minerals, the oat bran can then be sprinkled over breakfast cereals and mixed into plain or fruit yogurt to boost the fibre content. For best results, oat bran should be eaten daily at regular intervals. It can be a useful way to ease constipation and generally ensure that we are getting enough fibre in our diets.

Below: Add beta-glucan-rich oatmeal to dishes for slower-release energy.

CAN COELIACS EAT OATS?

This is a very common query for coeliac sufferers. It is important to note that oats do still contain a type of protein called avenin, which is similar to gluten and can cause a reaction in coeliacs, so oats should not automatically be considered as gluten-free.

Barley

Believed to be the oldest cultivated grain, barley is still a fundamental part of the everyday diet in Eastern Europe, the Middle East and Asia. Pearl barley, the most usual form, is husked, steamed and then polished to give it its characteristic ivory-coloured appearance. It has a mild, sweet flavour and chewy texture, and can be added to soups, stews and bakes. It is also used to make old-fashioned barley water. Pot barley is the whole grain with just the inedible outer husk removed. It takes much longer to cook than pearl barley. Pot barley is more nutritious than pearl barley, because it contains the extra soluble fibre, phosphorus, iron, magnesium, zinc and B vitamins, especially thiamin from the whole grain. More recently, studies have shown that its soluble fibre is the same as that found in oats – beta-glucan – and can have the same effect on reducing blood cholesterol levels. Barley flakes made from rolled whole barley are also available and make a good porridge or can be added to home-made muesli. Barley and barley-containing foods also have a good glycaemic index as they release their energy slowly.

Quinoa

Hailed as a true supergrain, quinoa (pronounced 'keen-wa') was called 'the mother grain' by the Incas, who cultivated it for hundreds of years. Quinoa's supergrain status hails from its rich nutritional value. Unlike other grains, quinoa contains a high level of

Above: Quinoa is a useful source of protein for vegetarians and vegans.

Above: Boil millet in milk for a sweet iron- and vitamin-B-rich porridge.

Above: Amaranth seeds contain an impressive list of nutrients.

protein, with a good balance of all of the essential amino acids, unusual for a food of vegetable origin. It is an excellent source of manganese, magnesium, copper, phosphorus, iron and zinc as well as B vitamins and insoluble fibre. It is particularly valuable for people with coeliac disease, as it is gluten-free. The tiny, bead-shaped grains have a mild, slightly bitter taste and firm texture. It is cooked in the same way as rice, but the grains quadruple in size, becoming translucent. Quinoa is useful for making stuffings, pilaffs, bakes and breakfast cereals.

Millet
Although millet is usually associated with bird food, it is a highly nutritious grain. It once rivalled barley as the main food of Europe and remains a staple ingredient in many parts of the world, including Africa, China and India. Millet is an easily digestible grain. It contains more iron than other grains and is a good source of manganese, copper, phosphorus, magnesium, and B vitamins, notably thiamin and niacin. Millet is gluten-free, so it is a useful food for people with coeliac disease. Its mild flavour makes it an ideal accompaniment to spicy stews and curries, and it can be used as a base for pilaffs or milk puddings. The tiny, firm grains can also be flaked or ground into flour. The flour can be used for baking, but

needs to be combined with high-gluten flours to make leavened bread; alternatively, it can make good flat bread. Toast the millet grain for an extra nutty flavour.

Buckwheat
In spite of its name, buckwheat is not a type of wheat, but is actually related to the rhubarb family. It is also very nutritious, containing all of the essential amino acids, minerals and B vitamins, especially niacin. Buckwheat also contains rutin, a flavonoid and antioxidant which has the ability to strengthen blood vessels and may help people with circulation problems. Buckwheat is gluten-free, and so is useful for people who suffer from coeliac disease.

The grain is available plain or toasted and it has a nutty, earthy flavour. It is a staple food in Eastern Europe as well as Russia, where the triangular grain is milled into a speckled-grey flour and used to make blini pancakes. Buckwheat pancakes are popular in parts of the USA and France. The whole grain, which is also known as kasha, makes a fine porridge or a creamy pudding. Buckwheat pasta made from buckwheat flour tastes nutty and is darker in colour than wholewheat pasta. Buckwheat noodles, of which soba noodles are the best-known type, are a much darker colour than wheat noodles –

almost grey. In Japan, soba noodles are traditionally served in soups or stir-fries with a variety of sauces.

Amaranth
This plant, which is native to Mexico, is unusual in that it can be eaten as both a vegetable and a grain. Like quinoa, amaranth is considered a supergrain due to its excellent nutritional content. Although its taste may take some getting used to, its nutritional qualities more than make up for it. Amaranth has more protein than pulses and is rich in all essential amino acids, particularly lysine. It is also high in B-vitamins, manganese, magnesium, phosphorus iron and zinc. Amaranth also contains calcium, but the high oxalic acid levels bind this and make it largely bio-unavailable. Amaranth is a natural source of plant stanols, which are chemically similar to phytosterols and have the same effect of reducing levels of the 'bad' LDL cholesterol, which may aid heart health. The tiny pale seed or 'grain' has a strong and distinctive, peppery flavour. It is best used in stews and soups or to make a porridge, but can also be ground into flour to make bread, pastries and cookies. The flour is gluten-free and has to be mixed with wheat or another flour that contains gluten to make leavened bread. Amaranth leaves are similar to spinach, but are less widely available,

LEGUMES

Extremely important in agriculture, legumes have the ability to fix nitrogen from the air and replenish the soil's nitrogen levels, which reduces the need for expensive fertilizers. Pulses are the seeds of these leguminous plants and are nutritionally vital, especially where meat production is limited or communities are vegetarian or vegan. Lentils and beans provide the cook with a diverse range of flavours and textures. They have long been a staple food in India, South America, the Middle East and the Mediterranean, and there is hardly a country that does not have its own favourite legume-based dish, from Boston baked beans in the USA to lentil dhal in India. In Mexico, they are spiced and used to make refried beans, while in China they are fermented for black bean sauces. Low in fat and high in complex carbohydrates, vitamins and minerals, legumes are also an important source of protein for vegetarians and, when eaten with cereals, easily match animal-based sources. The phytonutrient content of legumes is varied and the combined effect of this makes them a very valuable food to us – so much so

Below: High-fibre brown lentils take longer to cook than split varieties.

that the American dietary guidelines include a specific recommendation to consume as many as six portions of legumes per week.

Lentils

The humble lentil is one of our oldest wholefoods. It originated in Asia and North Africa and continues to be cultivated in those regions, as well as in France and Italy. Lentils have an impressive range of nutrients, including B vitamins, and are especially rich in folate; they also contain many essential minerals, including manganese, phosphorus, zinc, magnesium and copper. Lentils are one of the richest plant sources of iron, and even though it is in a form that is not easily absorbed, the high levels still make it a valuable contributor, especially in vegetarian and vegan diets. Extremely low in fat and richer in protein than most pulses, lentils contain both insoluble and soluble fibre. This insoluble fibre content aids the functioning of the bowels and colon and the soluble fibre reduces the 'bad' LDL cholesterol in the body. The fibre also slows down the rate at which sugar enters the bloodstream, providing a steady supply of energy, which could help reduce the risk of Type II diabetes. Lentils are not a complete source of protein as they do not contain all of the essential amino acids, but if they are served with a grain such as rice, this will make the dish a complete source. Phytonutrients present in lentils include flavonoids, isoflavones, phytosterols and lignans, all of which combine to make lentils a well-qualified superfood. This potent combination could be the reason why those with diets high in legumes have a lower incidence of Type II diabetes and cardiovascular disease. Lentils are hard even when fresh, so they are always sold dried. Unlike most other pulses, they do not need soaking. Although lentils can be kept for up to a year, they do toughen with time. Buy from shops with a

fast turnover of stock and store in airtight containers in a cool, dark place. Look for bright, unwrinkled pulses that are not dusty and always rinse well before use.

COOKING SPLIT RED AND YELLOW LENTILS

Lentils are easy to cook and do not need to be soaked beforehand. Split red and green lentils cook down to a soft consistency, while whole lentils retain their shape when cooked, but take longer to prepare.

1 Place 250g/9oz/generous 1 cup split lentils in a sieve (strainer) and rinse under cold running water. Transfer to a pan.

2 Cover with 600ml/1 pint/2½ cups water and bring to the boil. Simmer for 20–25 minutes, stirring occasionally, until the water is absorbed and the lentils are tender. Season to taste.

Red Lentils

Orange-coloured red split lentils, sometimes known as Egyptian lentils, are the most familiar variety. They cook in just 20 minutes, eventually disintegrating into a thick purée. They are ideal for thickening soups and casseroles and, when cooked with spices, make a delicious dhal. In the Middle East, red or yellow lentils are cooked and mixed with vegetables and spices to form balls known as kofte.

Yellow Lentils

Less well-known, yellow lentils taste very similar to the red variety and are used in much the same way and break down to a purée. Like red lentils, yellow lentils are split and therefore will not sprout.

Green and Brown Lentils

Sometimes referred to as continental lentils, these disc-shaped pulses retain their shape when cooked. Green and brown lentils contain

Below: Red lentils have less fibre than green varieties but cook faster.

Above: Fibre-dense green lentils absorb flavours such as garlic well.

30 per cent fibre, far higher than the 11 per cent found in red and yellow varieties. This means that they will take longer to cook than split lentils – about 40–45 minutes – and are ideal for adding to warm salads, casseroles and stuffings.

Puy Lentils

These tiny, dark, blue-green, marbled lentils grow in the Auvergne region of central France. They are considered to be far superior in taste and texture than other varieties, and they retain

Below: Iron-rich Puy lentils are a great accompaniment to fish dishes.

their bead-like shape during cooking, which takes around 25–30 minutes. Puy lentils are a delicious addition to simple dishes such as warm salads, and are also good braised in wine and flavoured with fresh herbs.

CREAMY RED LENTIL DHAL
This makes a tasty and satisfying winter supper for vegetarians and meat eaters alike. Serve with naan bread, coconut cream and fresh coriander (cilantro) leaves. The coconut cream gives this dish a really rich taste.

Serves 4
15ml/1 tbsp sunflower oil
500g/1¼lb/2 cups red lentils
15ml/1 tbsp hot curry paste
salt and ground black pepper

1 Heat the oil in a large pan and add the lentils. Fry for 1–2 minutes, stirring constantly, then stir in the curry paste and 600ml/ 1 pint/2½ cups boiling water.

2 Bring the mixture to the boil, then reduce the heat to a gentle simmer. Cover the pan and cook for 15 minutes, stirring occasionally, until the lentils are tender and the mixture has thickened.

3 Season the dhal with plenty of salt and ground black pepper to taste, and serve piping hot.

PULSES

Including chickpeas and a vast range of beans, these are the edible seeds from plants belonging to the legume family of pulses. They are packed with protein, vitamins, minerals and fibre, and are also extremely low in fat. Pulses count towards part of your target of eating five portions of fruit and vegetables a day. The protein contained in them is extremely good quality as it contains all of the essential amino acids, which is particularly valuable for vegetarian and vegan diets. Pulses are also rich in phytonutrients such as flavonoids, phytosterols and lignans, and studies show that people with diets rich in these nutrients have lower incidences of cardiovascular disease and Type II diabetes.

For the cook, their ability to absorb the flavours of other foods means that pulses can be used as the basis for an infinite number of dishes.

HOW TO PREPARE AND COOK PULSES

There is much debate as to whether soaking pulses before cooking is necessary, but it certainly reduces cooking times, and can enhance flavour by starting the germination process.

First, wash pulses under cold running water, then put in a bowl of fresh cold water and leave to soak overnight. Discard any pulses that float to the surface, drain and rinse again. Place the pulses in a large pan and cover with fresh cold water. Boil rapidly for 10–15 minutes, then reduce the heat, cover and simmer until tender.

Using a pressure cooker to cook pulses also reduces the cooking time by about two-thirds. Soak first as per usual, then follow your appliance's instructions. Timings are usually only about 20 minutes.

PULSE TIPS

Many people are put off eating beans due to their unfortunate side effects. The propensity of beans to cause flatulence stems from the gases they produce in the gut. Following these guidelines can reduce this:
• Never cook pulses in their soaking water as it contains indigestible sugars.
• Skim off any scum that forms on the surface of the water during cooking.
• Add digestive spices, such as dill, asafoetida, ginger, cumin and caraway, to the cooking water.

Most pulses require soaking overnight in cold water before use, so it is wise to plan ahead if using the dried type or alternatively, if you are pushed for time, many are available canned.

Black Beans

These shiny, black, kidney-shaped beans are often used in Caribbean cooking and are sometimes known as the black turtle bean. They are packed with nutrients, and are a very rich source of folate, which is particularly important if you are thinking of becoming or are pregnant, as it reduces the risk of neural tube defects in babies. Black beans are an

Above: Chickpeas are an excellent provider of protein and B-vitamins.

excellent source of all the B vitamins, which are essential for energy release and required for healthy nerves and muscles. They also contain good levels of all of the essential minerals, while remaining low in sodium. They do contain iron and calcium, but these will be bound with phytates and are less bioavailable. The beans have a sweetish flavour, and their colour adds a dramatic touch to soups, salads or casseroles.

Chickpeas

Also known as garbanzo beans, robust and hearty chickpeas resemble shelled hazelnuts, and have a delicious nutty flavour together with a creamy texture. As with black beans, the protein in chickpeas is very high quality and contains all of the essential amino acids. Chickpeas are an extremely rich source of folate, and the other B-vitamins are also well represented. They have a valuable array of essential minerals, including a modest amount of calcium, useful if you don't or can't have dairy products in your diet. They are a good source of insoluble fibre, improving bulk and preventing

Left: Black beans are a good source of folate and other B vitamins.

constipation, which could reduce the risk of colon cancer. This fibre content also contributes to a good glycaemic index, which can help manage diabetes and may even reduce cholesterol levels. They do need lengthy cooking if you are using dried chickpeas, however, canned ones are available which are more convenient. Chickpeas taste excellent in curries, and make a wonderful creamy hummus dip which can be flavoured with ingredients such as pesto, coriander (cilantro), lemon or roasted peppers.

Red Kidney Beans

Glossy, mahogany-red kidney beans retain their colour and kidney shape when cooked. They are not quite a

Above: High in protein and fibre, kidney beans add colour to cooking.

complete protein as some essential amino acids are missing; however, combining with a cereal or grain food will complement the profile and make it complete. Red beans and rice is one such classic combination. They contain high levels of folate, manganese, phosphorus and iron and are a good source of both soluble and insoluble fibre, both of which reduce cardiovascular risk by lowering cholesterol and improving the glycaemic index of food. Kidney beans have a soft, 'mealy' texture and are much used in South American cooking. An essential ingredient in spicy chillies, they can also be used to make refried beans (although this dish is traditionally made from pinto beans).

Cooked kidney beans can be used to make a variety of salads, but they taste especially good when combined with red onion and chopped flat leaf parsley and mint, then tossed in an olive oil dressing.

It is essential to follow cooking guidelines when preparing dried kidney beans. You should always boil them vigorously for 10–15 minutes in order to destroy the harmful substances called lectins, which cause a severe food-poisoning reaction of nausea, vomiting and diarrhoea as

THE MANTECA BEAN

The American space programme NASA is involved in research into flatulence-free foods. One such food is the manteca bean, also known as the Jersey yellow bean, discovered in Chile by British scientist Dr Colin Leakey. This small, yellow bean is flatulence-free and easy to digest. The bean is now being grown both in Cambridgeshire, England, and the Channel Islands, and should become more widely available.

COOKING KIDNEY BEANS

Most types of beans, with the exception of aduki beans and mung beans, require soaking for 5–6 hours or overnight and then boiling rapidly for 10–15 minutes to remove any harmful toxins. This is particularly important for kidney beans, which can cause serious food poisoning if not treated in this way.

1 Wash the beans well, then place in a bowl that allows plenty of room for expansion. Cover with cold water and leave to soak overnight or for 8–12 hours, then drain and rinse.

2 Place the beans in a large pan and cover with fresh cold water. Bring to the boil and boil rapidly for 10–15 minutes, then reduce the heat and simmer for 1–1½ hours, until the beans are tender. Drain and serve.

they damage the cell lining of the gut. Canned kidney beans have already been cooked, so they can be used safely from the can and either heated up or served cold.

SOYA BEANS

These small, oval beans vary in colour from creamy-yellow through brown to black. In China, they are known as 'meat of the earth' and were once considered sacred. Soya beans are the most nutritious of all the beans, being rich in high-quality protein. This wonder-pulse contains all of the essential amino acids that cannot be synthesized by the body but are vital for the renewal of cells and tissues. They are high in insoluble fibre, ensuring regular bowel movements, while the soluble fibre and the soya phytoestrogens associated with the protein have been found to lower blood cholesterol, thereby reducing the risk of heart disease and stroke. They are a good source of vegetarian omega-3 and a-linolenic acid, which is an important source if you do not include fish in your diet.

The phytoestrogen content has also been associated with reducing the symptoms of the menopause, but this effect has not been scientifically proven. The combination of many excellent nutritional factors in the soya bean makes this food of great value and interest to us. It is also processed into other foods that retain these benefits and make it a more versatile, bioavailable food. Soya beans are extremely dense and need to be soaked for 12 hours before cooking or, to save time, can be cooked in a pressure cooker in larger batches and then frozen. They combine well with robust ingredients such as garlic, herbs and spices, and they make a healthy addition to soups, casseroles, bakes and salads.

The Goodness of Soya

The American FDA among others have approved a heart-health claim stating that 25g/1oz of soya protein per day, as part of a diet low in saturated fat and cholesterol, may reduce the risk of heart disease.

Green Soya Beans

These differ from the light creamy brown variety only in age. These are the young beans, picked before they fully ripen to become mature

---

USING CANNED BEANS

Canned beans are convenient store-cupboard standbys, as they don't require soaking or lengthy cooking. Choose canned beans that do not have added sugar or salt, and rinse well and drain before use. The canning process reduces the levels of vitamins and minerals, but canned beans still contain reputable amounts. Canned beans tend to be softer than cooked, dried beans, so they are easy to mash, which makes them good for pâtés, stuffings, croquettes and rissoles, but they can also be used to make quick salads. They can, in fact, be used for any dish that calls for cooked, dried beans: a drained 425g/15oz can is roughly the equivalent of 150g/5oz/¾ cup dried beans. Firmer canned beans, such as kidney beans, can be added to stews and re-cooked, but softer beans such as flageolet should be merely heated through.

BEAN TIPS

- If you are short of time, the long soaking process can be speeded up. First, cook the beans in boiling water for 2 minutes, then remove the pan from the heat. Cover and leave for about 2 hours. Drain, rinse and cover with plenty of fresh cold water before cooking.
- Cooking beans in a pressure cooker will reduce the cooking time by around three-quarters.
- Do not add salt to beans while they are cooking, as this will cause them to toughen. Cook the beans first, then season with salt and pepper. Acidic foods such as tomatoes, lemons or vinegar will also toughen beans, so only add these ingredients once the beans are soft.

Above: Phytonutrient-rich soya beans can be eaten whole in their pods.

soya beans. Traditionally in Japan the whole pod is picked, boiled and then served with salt. This dish is known as 'edamame' and is a popular snack food. More recently, these green soya beans, which are sometimes known as edamame beans, have become available as a fresh or frozen bean. They can be eaten as an alternative to other green vegetables such as peas or broad beans. They are highly nutritious and are an excellent source of high-quality protein, containing all of the essential amino acids; however, unfortunately, they do not contain many vegetarian omega-3 fats, unlike their older soya bean siblings. They do enjoy the same advantage of containing the isoflavones group of phytonutrients, which are responsible for the highly researched area of cholesterol reduction and the subsequent benefits to heart health. Thus, the inclusion of these little green beans can significantly contribute to your diet if you are trying to reduce cholesterol levels.

Green soya beans are quite firm and so will require boiling for a little longer than other beans or peas. Their firmness, however, makes them perfect for including in salads and cold dishes as they do not turn at all mushy. They even taste delicious on their own, dressed simply with a little vinaigrette.

QUICK COOKING AND SERVING IDEAS FOR PULSES

- To flavour beans, add an onion, garlic, herbs or spices before cooking. Remove whole flavourings before serving.

- Dress cooked beans with extra virgin olive oil, lemon juice, crushed garlic, diced tomato and fresh basil.

- Mash cooked beans with olive oil, garlic and coriander (cilantro), and pile on to toasted bread. Top with a poached egg.

- Spoon spicy, red lentil dhal and some crisp, fried onions on top of a warm tortilla, then roll it up and eat immediately.

- Mix cooked chickpeas with spring onions (scallions), olives and chopped parsley, then drizzle over olive oil and lemon juice.

- Roast cooked chickpeas, which have been drizzled with olive oil and garlic, for 20 minutes at 200°C/400°F/Gas 6, then toss in a little ground cumin and sprinkle with chilli flakes. Serve with chunks of feta cheese and wam naan bread.

- Gently fry cooked red kidney beans in olive oil with chopped onion, chilli, garlic and fresh coriander (cilantro) leaves.

SOYA BEAN PRODUCTS

The soya bean is the most nutritious of all the beans and these credentials are mostly preserved when the bean is used to make other products that can be used in cooking. Examples of these products include tofu, tempeh, textured vegetable protein, flour, miso and a variety of sauces. Some of these are produced by a process of fermenting the soya beans, which actually enhances the phytonutrient bioavailability. All of these products do still contain soya protein, which importantly has the soya isoflavones associated with them. This has the approval of the FDA and other similar organizations to carry the health claim: '25g of soya protein per day, as part of a diet low in saturated fat and cholesterol may reduce the risk of heart disease'. Vegetarian omega-3 fats are still found in soya products – the amount varies according to the fat content of the food.

Tofu

Also known as beancurd, tofu is made in a similar way to soft cheese. The beans are boiled, mashed and sieved (strained) to make soya 'milk', and the 'milk' is then curdled using a

Below: Firm tofu provides good amounts of vegetarian omega-3 fats.

coagulant. The resulting curds are drained and pressed to make tofu, and there are several different types to choose from. All varieties of fresh tofu can be stored in the refrigerator for up to one week.

Firm Tofu

This type of tofu is sold in blocks and can be cubed or sliced and used in vegetable stir-fries, kebabs, salads, soups and casseroles. Alternatively, firm tofu can be mashed and used in bakes and burgers. Tofu is a good source of vegetarian omega-3 fats, and sometimes calcium sulphate is used as a firming agent, which makes it a good source of calcium. The bland flavour of firm tofu is improved by marinating, because its porous texture readily absorbs flavours and seasonings. Firm tofu should be kept covered in water, which must be changed regularly. Freezing tofu is not recommended because it alters the texture.

Silken Tofu

Soft with a silky, smooth texture, this type of tofu is ideal for use in sauces, dressings, dips and soups. It is a useful dairy-free alternative to cream, soft cheese or yogurt, and

Below: Silken tofu has fewer omega-3 fats than firm, but has plenty of protein.

TOFU FRUIT FOOL

1 Place a packet of silken tofu in the bowl of a food processor. Add some soft fruit or berries – for example, strawberries, raspberries or blackberries.

2 Process the mixture to form a smooth purée, then sweeten to taste with a little honey, maple syrup or maize malt syrup.

can be used to make creamy desserts. As it has a lower fat content, it is not as good a source of vegetarian omega-3 fats as firm tofu. Silken tofu is often available in long-life vacuum packs, which do not have to be kept in the refrigerator and have a much longer shelf life.

Other Forms of Tofu

Smoked, marinated and deep-fried tofu are all readily available in health food stores and Asian shops, as well as in some supermarkets. Deep-fried tofu is fairly tasteless, but it has an interesting texture. It puffs up during cooking and underneath the golden, crisp coating the tofu is white and soft, and easily absorbs the flavour of other ingredients. It can be used in much the same way as firm tofu and, as it has been fried in vegetable oil, it is suitable for vegetarian cooking.

Tempeh

This Indonesian speciality is made by fermenting cooked soya beans with a cultured starter forming a soya

'cake'. This concentrated soya
product is high in protein, B-vitamins
and minerals and retains its level of
vegetarian omega-3 fats. It is much
more easily digested due to the
fermentation process, and is a
complete protein source containing
all the essential amino acids we need
to maintain health. Many consider
it to be an excellent alternative to
meat, as the firmer texture of
tempeh means that it can be used in
pies and casseroles. Tempeh is similar
to tofu but has a nuttier, more
savoury flavour. It can be used in the
same way as firm tofu and also
benefits from marinating. Tempeh is
available from health food stores.
Chilled tempeh can be stored in the

*Below: Textured vegetable protein
(TVP) is a versatile meat replacement.*

refrigerator for up to a week. Frozen
tempeh can be left in the freezer for
one month; defrost before use.

TVP
Textured vegetable protein, or TVP
as it is commonly referred to is a
useful meat replacement usually
bought in mince form or as dry
chunks. Made from processed soya
beans, TVP is very versatile and
readily absorbs the strong flavours
of ingredients such as herbs, spices
and vegetable stock. It is very high
in protein and low in fat and sodium;
however, it is not a good source
of vegetarian omega-3 fats as it is
virtually fat-free. TVP is inexpensive
and is a convenient store-cupboard
item. It does need to be rehydrated
in boiling water or vegetable stock,
and can be used in stews and
curries, or as a filling for pies.

Miso
This thick paste is made from a
mixture of cooked soya beans, rice,
wheat or barley, salt and water
which is then left to ferment for up
to three years. This concentrated soya
product has a good nutrient profile
containing the all-important soya
isoflavones as well as good levels of
B vitamins and minerals. However, it
is very high in sodium and so should
be used sparingly. It is reputed that,
in the past, miso has helped people
with radiation sickness and may have
some cancer-reducing properties, but
this has not been conclusively proven.
Miso is primarily used as a flavouring
to add a savoury flavour to soups,
stocks, stir-fries and noodle dishes,
and is a staple food in Asia. There are
three main types: kome, or hite miso,
is the lightest and sweetest; medium-
strength mugi miso, which has a
mellow flavour and is preferred for
everyday use; and hacho miso, which
is a dark chocolate colour, and has a
thick texture and a strong flavour.
Miso can be stored for several
months, but should be kept in the
refrigerator once it has been opened.

Soya Milk and Soya Milk Produce
Soya milk and soya milk products are
the most widely used alternatives to
milk and dairy products. Made from
pulverized soya beans, soya milk is
suitable for both cooking and
drinking and is used to make cheese,
yogurt and cream. Soya milk is very
similar in nutritional value to cow's
milk, and is an excellent source of
protein, iron, magnesium,
phosphorus and vitamin E. Unlike
cow's milk, however, it is also a good
source of soya isoflavones. The 'milk'
is low in calories and contains no
cholesterol. The calcium naturally
present in the soya milk is largely bio-
unavailable, bound up by phytates;
however, many soya milks are
fortified with calcium to compensate
for this. Soya milk is often used as
a milk alternative, especially among
sufferers of lactose intolerance.
Soya cream is made from a higher
proportion of beans than that in soya
milk, which gives it a richer flavour
and thicker texture. It has a similar
consistency to single cream and can
be used in the same ways. Most soya
milks and creams are sold in long-life
cartons, so they do not require
refrigeration until opened. Try to buy
unsweetened soya milk if possible.

*Below: Soya milk is often fortified
with calcium and vitamin D.*

Nuts

With the exception of peanuts, nuts are the storage fruits of trees and are therefore full of nutrients and oils, being particularly rich in B vitamins, vitamin E, potassium, magnesium, calcium, phosphorus and iron. Nuts are also a good source of fibre and phytosterols, and most contain mainly unsaturated fat. There is mounting evidence that the regular consumption of nuts (25g/1oz, five times or more a week) is associated with a reduced risk of cardiovascular disease due to the effect on 'bad' LDL cholesterol, and Type II diabetes due to their low glycaemic index. Nuts are particularly important for vegetarians and vegans because of their abundance of nutrients, although they contain a hefty number of calories. The quality and availability of fresh nuts can vary with the seasons, although most types are sold dried, either whole or prepared ready for use. Always buy nuts in small quantities from a shop with a high turnover of stock, because if kept for too long, they can turn rancid. Nuts in their shells should feel heavy for their size. Store nuts in airtight containers in a cool, dark

Below: Eating a handful of mixed nuts is an ideal nutritious snack.

NUT ALLERGY
Any food has the potential to cause an allergic reaction, but peanuts, as well as walnuts, Brazil nuts, hazelnuts and almonds are also known to be allergens. In cases of extreme allergy, nuts can trigger a life-threatening reaction known as anaphylaxis. Symptoms include facial swelling, shortness of breath, dizziness and loss of consciousness, so it is essential that sufferers take every precaution to avoid nuts.

place or in the refrigerator and they should maintain their freshness for at least three months.

Almonds
There are two types of almonds, sweet and bitter. Sweet almonds are not actually sweetened but are so called as a way of differentiating them from bitter almonds, which are used to make essences and oil. Bitter almonds should never be eaten raw as they contain a poisonous acid. Almonds are a very good source of fibre, phytosterols and unsaturated fat and, as well as being a good

Above: Almonds provide an excellent source of calcium.

source of B vitamins, are packed with all of the essential minerals, especially manganese, magnesium and copper. Studies have shown that eating almonds regularly can increase 'good' HDL cholesterol and reduce 'bad' LDL cholesterol, and therefore may reduce heart-disease risk. Ground almonds can be used as a substitute for part of the flour content of cake and biscuit (cookie) recipes, and because they have almost no carbohydrate content, will reduce the glycaemic index and release energy more slowly. Sweet almonds are widely available as ground, flaked, toasted flaked, blanched (skins off), slithers and whole forms. Each form has its own traditional use, from making marzipan with ground almonds to topping cakes and biscuits with flaked almonds.

Brazil Nuts
These are, in fact, seeds, and are grown mainly in the Amazon regions of Brazil and other neighbouring countries. Between 12 and 20 Brazil nuts grow, packed snugly together in a large brown husk, hence their three-cornered wedge shape. They have a very high fat content at around 70 per cent, contain the largest amount of saturated fat of all of the nuts,

MAKING NUT BUTTER
Shop-bought nut butters often contain unwanted hydrogenated oil and can be loaded with sugar. To avoid additives, make your own butter using a combination of peanuts, hazelnuts and cashew nuts.

1 Place 75g/3oz/½ cup shelled nuts in a food processor or blender and process until finely and evenly ground.

2 Pour 15–30ml/1–2 tbsp of sunflower oil into the processor or blender and process to a coarse paste. Store in an airtight jar.

and will go rancid very quickly. They have an extraordinarily high level of selenium, one of the highest levels known in foods. Selenium is not just an essential mineral but a powerful antioxidant that has been studied extensively in the area of cancer prevention. Selenium is involved in many metabolic processes including eliminating potentially damaging free radicals, which is especially significant in areas such as the protection of developing sperm in men. Selenium is also involved in ensuring that the

Above: Brazil nuts are one of the best known sources of selenium.

immune system functions properly, and may also help to prevent cancer, because populations with low selenium intake have higher cancer death rates for diseases such as prostate cancer. More evidence is needed, however, to prove any connection with a higher selenium consumption and the prevention of cancer. Brazil nuts have quite an earthy flavour and work well in baked items such as cookies, but can also be used to make pesto or nut butters.

Chestnuts
Not to be confused with the horse chestnut (conker) variety, the sweet chestnut is edible and surprisingly, unlike other nuts, chestnuts are very low in fat (about 1 per cent). Sweet chestnuts are an autumnal crop and it is not uncommon to see people foraging for these. Out of season, chestnuts can be bought dried, canned or puréed. Raw chestnuts are not recommended as they are not only unpleasant to eat but also contain tannic acid, which inhibits the absorption of iron. However, antioxidant-rich chestnuts taste excellent when roasted, which complements their soft, floury texture. Try adding whole chestnuts to winter stews, soups, stuffings or pies, or even cakes. Chestnuts are preserved in syrup to make the famous marrons glacé.

Above: Surprisingly, chestnuts contain only 1 per cent fat.

Peanuts
Not strictly a nut, but a member of the pulse family, peanuts bury themselves just below the earth after flowering – hence their alternative name, groundnuts. Peanuts are particularly high in fat but it is mainly of the monounsaturated and

ROASTING AND SKINNING NUTS
The flavour of most nuts, particularly hazelnuts and peanuts, is improved by roasting. It also enables the thin outer skin to be removed more easily.

1 Place the nuts in a single layer on a baking sheet. Bake at 180°C/350°F/Gas 4 for 10–20 minutes, or until the skins begin to split and the nuts are golden.

2 Transfer the nuts to a dish towel and rub to loosen and remove the skins.

polyunsaturated types. They are a good source of vitamin E and the B vitamins, especially niacin and folate, and are an excellent source of all of the essential minerals. Their vitamin E content, along with polyphenols such as coumaric acid, contributes to an excellent antioxidant profile, rivalling that of many fruits and vegetables. More recently, it has been discovered that peanuts also contain a high concentration of phytosterols, notably resveratrol. This compound has been shown in animal studies to reduce both cancer and cardiovascular disease risk, and may have an impact on the ageing of the body; however, research in humans is inconclusive at the moment. Buy unsalted peanuts for use in cooking as salted peanuts will be much higher in sodium, which could counteract any potential heart-health benefits. Peanuts are good in both sweet and savoury dishes, and can be made into sauces or put into stews.

Pistachio Nuts

Incredibly moreish when served as a snack, pistachio nuts have pale green flesh and thin, reddish-purple skin. Sold shelled or in a split shell, these mild nuts are often used chopped as a colourful garnish or sprinkled over both sweet and savoury foods. As with most nuts they are high in fat;

Below: Protein-packed peanuts make a handy on-the-go snack.

Above: Pistachio nuts are high in the antioxidant vitamin E.

however, they also have high levels of antioxidants such as lutein, beta-carotene and tocopherol (vitamin E). This antioxidant content has caught the eye of researchers who are investigating the potential for pistachios to help reduce the 'bad' LDL cholesterol and therefore reduce the risk of heart disease.

Check before buying pistachio nuts for cooking, as they are often sold salted, which would potentially negate any positive benefits. Traditionally used in many sweet dishes, especially those of Arabic origin, pistachios have a fabulous green colour which is unusual in sweet dishes. Pistachios can also be used in savoury dishes such as

Below: Walnuts have the highest vegetable omega-3 levels of all nuts.

stuffing and on salads, ground up and sprinkled on dishes as a garnish or just eaten as a snack.

Walnuts

Most walnuts are imported from France, Italy and California, but they are also grown in the Middle East, Britain and China. They are the only nut with significant quantities of vegetarian omega-3 and are also high in antioxidants. These two factors are thought to contribute to the cardio-protective properties of walnuts; they have been shown to reduce inflammation of arteries and reduce the oxidative stress on the artery wall, leading to less tissue damage. Walnuts also contain a high proportion of arginine, an amino acid that the body uses to produce chemicals that keep blood vessels flexible, also contributing to heart health. Walnuts have also been studied for their effects on Alzheimer's disease, where walnut extracts have been shown to reduce the presence of 'plaques' in the brains of sufferers, and this may delay the onset of the disease. Walnuts are an excellent source of folate, thiamin and vitamin B6 as well as containing an excellent range of minerals in significant quantities. Dried walnuts have a delicious bittersweet flavour, and can be bought shelled, chopped or ground. They can be used to make excellent cakes and biscuits (cookies) as well as rich pie fillings, but are also good added to savoury dishes such as stir-fries and salads – the classic Waldorf salad mixes whole kernels with celery and apples in a mayonnaise dressing.

Cocoa

The cocoa bean originates from the Amazon basin, where the indigenous populations have consumed cocoa for many hundreds of years, recognizing its benefits to health. In more recent years, it has been revealed that cocoa has high levels of antioxidants as well as containing

HOW MUCH COCOA IS IN CHOCOLATE?

Chocolate products should indicate on their labels the percentage of cocoa solids that they contain. The higher the percentage, the more cocoa the product contains and the darker and more bitter the chocolate.

Percentages greater than 75 per cent are usually termed 'continental chocolate' and are excellent for baking and melting for sauces or toppings. Products at 45 per cent or less are usually cheaper milk chocolate products and are best for eating, as they are not strong enough to impart a good chocolate flavour in recipes. Chocolate with up to 90 per cent cocoa solids is available, which is very strong and bitter.

some very interesting amine compounds and tryptophan. These compounds are metabolized into neurotransmitters, which may be the reason why eating chocolate makes you feel good, or why it is a common comfort food, as they may have anti-depressant effects. Cocoa is also a good source of polyphenols similar to those found in red wine, and has been shown to reduce the 'bad' LDL cholesterol and raise the 'good' HDL cholesterol in the body. This, along with high levels of antioxidant activity, could contribute to a reduced cardiovascular risk. It is important to note, however, that the studies have been carried out on cocoa, not

Above: Add pure cocoa powder to recipes to boost antioxidant power.

chocolate, and so to get the most potential benefit, it is best to use a high cocoa solids product which is far more bitter than milk chocolate. Eating too much chocolate could lead to excess energy intake and therefore obesity.

Coconuts

These versatile nuts grow all over the tropics. Their white dense meat, or flesh, is made into desiccated coconut, blocks of creamed coconut and a thick and creamy milk.

Coconut flesh is over 50 per cent fat, most of which is saturated. It is the nature of this saturated fat that has been the subject of much interest and research. The saturated fat molecules in coconut are smaller than in most other saturated fats, and are known as medium chain triglycerides, or MCT's for short. These fats are absorbed into the body without having to go through the metabolism and breakdown that the larger saturated fat molecules do. This characteristic has led researchers to try to understand their impact on fat metabolism in the body. They have suggested that they may even help mobilize existing fat stores for energy and therefore actually lead to weight loss, which could help to combat the rise of obesity in the developed world. When buying a coconut, make sure that there is no sign of mould or a rancid smell. Give it a

Above: Coconut fat is more easily metabolized than most other fats.

shake – it should be full of liquid. Keep coconut milk in the refrigerator or freezer once opened. Store desiccated coconut in an airtight container, but don't store it for too long as its high fat content means that it is prone to rancidity.

COCONUT MILK

Available in cans or long-life cartons, coconut milk or cream is also easy to make at home: pour 225g/8oz/2⅔ cups desiccated coconut into a food processor, add 450ml/¾ pint/ scant 2 cups boiling water and process for 30 seconds. Leave to cool slightly. Pour into a sieve (strainer) lined with muslin (cheesecloth) and placed over a bowl. Gather the ends of the cloth. Twist the cloth to extract the liquid, then discard the spent coconut. Store the coconut milk in the refrigerator for 1–2 days, or freeze.

Seeds

They may be very small, but seeds are nutritional powerhouses, packed with vitamins and minerals, as well as beneficial oils and protein. They can be used in a huge array of sweet and savoury dishes, and will add an instant, healthy boost, pleasant crunch and nutty flavour when added to rice and pasta dishes, salads, stir-fries, soups and yogurt. All seeds are high in polyunsaturated fat, but being a healthier fat it means that they can go rancid more quickly, so keep in an airtight container in a cool dark place.

Sunflower Seeds
These are the seeds of the sunflower, a symbol of summer, and an important commercial crop throughout the world. The impressive, golden-yellow flowers are grown mainly for their seeds, which are then either processed for food use or pressed for their oil, which contains essential omega-6 fatty acids. The seeds are particularly rich in vitamin E and thiamin, and are a good source of B vitamins and the minerals manganese, copper, magnesium and selenium. These all contribute to sunflower seeds having a good level of antioxidant activity and, along with the phytosterols present, they

Below: Sweet, nutty pumpkin seeds contain high amounts of tryptophan.

can have a positive influence on cholesterol levels, which may lead to improved heart health. Sunflower seeds are also a good source of tryptophan, an essential amino acid required by the body to make, among other things, serotonin and melatonin. These are important chemicals in the brain that affect how we control our mood and metabolism. The pale-green, tear-drop-shaped seeds have a semi-crunchy texture and an oily taste that is much improved by dry-roasting or toasting. Sprinkle sunflower seeds over salads, rice pilaffs and couscous, or use in bread dough, muffins, casseroles and baked dishes.

Pumpkin Seeds
Richer in iron than any other seed and an excellent source of manganese, magnesium and phosphorus, pumpkin seeds make a nutritious snack eaten on their own. They also contain the essential omega-6 and omega-3 fats, both important for heart health. Tryptophan is found in high levels, and this is essential for the production of serotonin and melatonin, which control mood and influence our sleep patterns.

Below: A sprinkling of seeds adds an extra nutritional boost to smoothies.

ROASTING SEEDS
The flavour of seeds is much improved by 'roasting' them in a dry frying pan. Black poppy seeds won't turn golden brown, so watch them carefully to make sure that they don't scorch.

1 Spread out a spoonful or two of seeds in a thin layer in a large, non-stick frying pan, and heat them gently.

2 Cook over a medium heat for 2–3 minutes, tossing the seeds frequently, until they all turn golden brown.

In traditional medicine such as that of the Native Americans, pumpkin seeds were used to cure problems of the urinary tract. It is still not known how this may work, but clinical studies have given some credence to this attribute. This is also the case with pumpkins seeds' reputed ability to kill off intestinal parasites such as tapeworm. One particular area of ongoing research has focused on the steroid content of pumpkin seeds and their role in treating conditions such as prostate disorders. Pumpkin seeds are delicious lightly toasted, tossed in a little toasted sesame seed oil or soy sauce, or stirred into salads.

Flax seeds
Also known as linseeds, these small golden seeds are packed full of goodness. They are one of the best vegetarian sources of omega-3 fats.

Above: Crushing hemp seeds makes the nutrients more bioavailable to us.

Above: Flax seeds offer one of the best sources of vegetarian omega-3 fats.

Above: Heart-healthy psyllium is a very concentrated source of fibre.

They are very high in fibre and contain lignan, a type of phytoestrogen, which is converted by bacteria in the lower intestine into active compounds. These oestrogen-like compounds play an important role in cell signalling, which affects the way that the body controls areas such as bone density, hormonal processes and reproductive processes. Eating foods rich in lignans is consistently associated with a lower incidence of heart disease, and it is thought that it is the collective effect of all of the cardioprotective nutrients, rather than one in particular, that is responsible. Flax seeds have a very resistant outer hull, so in order to gain the most benefit, use ground flax seed to ensure that the body can absorb the goodness, otherwise the seeds will pass through it unaffected. Flax seeds have a pleasant nutty taste but, due to their high oil content, must be stored in a sealed container, preferably in the refrigerator, to prevent the oil from going rancid.

Hemp Seeds

These small round seeds have quite a hard shell. They can be bought whole or ground into a meal, the latter being more favourable as the shell can be difficult to eat. Their nutty flavour can be enhanced by roasting them carefully in a dry frying pan, and if you then grind them up, they can make a tasty topping or crust for

almost anything sweet or savoury. Hemp seeds contain an excellent array of amino acids, making them one of the most complete vegetarian sources of protein. The seed also contains all of the essential fatty acids required to maintain health, including vegetarian omega 3.

Psyllium

It is the seed husk of psyllium that is of most interest, as this is the highly fibrous part that contains the active components. The fibre is soluble in water and is able to absorb large quantities, making it useful for counteracting diarrhoea or helping with constipation. Indeed, it is found as the base ingredient in many over-the-counter-preparations. There have also been studies showing that psyllium can reduce total cholesterol, including 'bad' LDL cholesterol in the blood, thus helping to reduce the risk of heart disease. In the US, the FDA has approved a health claim to this effect when psyllium is used as part of a diet low in saturated fat and cholesterol, and this now appears on many 'fortified' products such as breakfast cereals. It is available in powdered form, which makes it easier to add to foods; however, due to its massive water-absorption capacity, it must be eaten with liquids or extra liquid must be added to the recipe. In a similar way to oats, psyllium can also slow energy release from foods

and not cause insulin spikes. This can help diabetics to improve control of the disease, but psyllium must be taken with the advice of a medical professional due to its laxative effects.

QUICK IDEAS FOR SEEDS
- Sprinkle over breads, cakes and biscuits (cookies) just before baking.
- Combine with dried or fresh fruit, chopped nuts and natural yogurt to make a delicious and nutritious breakfast.
- Add to flapjacks, wholemeal scones or pastry for a nutty taste.
- Add a spoonful of your favourite seeds to rissoles, casseroles or vegetable burgers.
- Mix with rolled oats, flour, butter or margarine, and sugar to make a sweet crumble topping. To make a savoury topping, omit the sugar and combine with chopped fresh or dried herbs.
- Use sunflower or pumpkin seeds in place of pine nuts to make pesto.
- Sprinkle seeds over a mixed green salad.
- Add an instant nutritional boost to vegetable stir-fries or noodle dishes, by sprinkling a handful of seeds over the top before serving.

Spices

Highly revered for thousands of years, spices – the seeds, fruit, pods, bark and buds of plants – have been valuable commodities, often traded as a currency. In addition to their ability to add flavour and interest to the most unassuming of ingredients, the evocative aroma of spices stimulates the appetite. Today spices are still prized for their reputed medicinal properties and culinary uses, and they play a vital role in creating healthy and appetizing cooking. Their health benefits are often attributed to the intense aromatic, volatile oils they contain. Similarly to herbs, these compounds have very high antioxidant activity, and spices have some of the highest recorded ORAC scores on record. Buy spices in small quantities from a shop with a regular turnover of stock. Aroma is the best indication of freshness, as this diminishes when the spice is stale. Store in airtight jars in a cool place away from direct light.

Ginger

This spice is probably one of the oldest and most popular herbal medicines, being cited in many remedies for nausea, colic and intestinal cramps. Ginger contains volatile phenols that give it its

---

PREPARING FRESH GINGER

1 Fresh root ginger is most easily peeled using a vegetable peeler or a small, sharp paring knife.

3 Grate ginger finely – special graters are available, but a box grater will do the job equally well.

2 Chop ginger using a sharp knife to the size specified in the recipe.

4 Freshly grated ginger can be squeezed to release the juice.

---

characteristic scent and flavour and contribute toward its phytonutrient activity. Gingerol is the active volatile involved in helping to prevent nausea. It is best to eat fresh ginger for nausea, as it is converted to zingerone and shogaol when cooked, which are less effective against nausea. These compounds are more useful for treating diarrhoea. Gingerol has also been shown to have some anti-inflammatory activity. The fresh root, which is spicy, peppery and fragrant, is good in both sweet and savoury dishes, adding a hot, yet refreshing, flavour to marinades, stir-fries, soups, and fresh vegetables. It also adds warmth to poached fruit, pastries and cakes. Ground ginger is the usual choice for flavouring cakes, cookies and other baked goods, but finely grated fresh ginger can also be used and is

equally good. Pink pickled ginger is finely sliced ginger that has been pickled in sugar and vinegar and is served as an accompaniment to Japanese food.

Below: The gingerol in fresh ginger helps to alleviate nausea.

GINGER TEA

This soothing tea is comforting for those suffering from nausea, colds, flu and stomach upsets.

1 To make ginger tea, roughly chop a 2.5cm/1in piece of fresh root ginger. Place in a cup and pour in boiling water.

2 Cover and leave for 7–10 minutes. Strain or drink as it is – the ginger will stay in the bottom of the cup.

Stem ginger is preserved in a thick sugar syrup and sold in jars. This sweet ginger can be chopped and used in desserts, or added to cake mixtures, steamed puddings, scones, shortbread and muffins. Fresh root ginger should look firm, thin-skinned and unblemished. Avoid withered, woody-looking roots, as these are likely to be dry and fibrous. Store in the refrigerator or freeze. Ground ginger should smell aromatic; keep in a cool, dark place.

Cardamom

Belonging to the ginger family, cardamom is often used in Middle Eastern and Indian cooking. It contains a volatile oil called cineole, which has the ability to help relieve congestion in the chest and alleviate cold symptoms. Cardamom also contains many other volatile oils, which contribute to its distinctive aroma and flavour and has been used for many years, chewed whole, to freshen the breath and calm indigestion. Cardamom is best bought whole in its pod, as it soon loses its aromatic flavour when ground. The pod can be used whole, slightly crushed, or for a more intense flavour, the seeds can be ground. This flavourful spice tastes superb in both sweet and savoury dishes. It can be infused in milk used

Below: The cineole in cardamom may help to reduce cold symptoms.

Above: Cinnamon helps to maintain healthy blood sugar levels.

to flavour rice pudding or ice cream, and is often added to curries and other Indian dishes.

Cinnamon

This warm, comforting spice is available in sticks (quills) and in ground form. As the bark is difficult to grind, it is useful to keep both forms in the store cupboard. Cinnamon sticks can enhance both sweet and savoury dishes and are widely used to flavour pilaffs, curries, and dried fruit compotes, but remember to remove before serving. Ground cinnamon adds a pleasing fragrance to cakes, cookies and fruit. Recently evidence has emerged that cinnamon may help people with Type II diabetes. The active components may help the insulin to metabolize sugar more efficiently and keep the blood sugar levels low and safe. It also has some effect on blood fats, reducing the 'bad' LDL cholesterol, and while it has not been shown to increase 'good' HDL cholesterol, the positive effect on the overall ratio is beneficial to diabetics.

Cumin

Extensively used in Indian curries, cumin is also a familiar component of Mexican, North African and Middle

Above: Dry-fry cumin seeds before crushing to release the essential oils.

Eastern cooking. The seeds have a robust aroma and slightly bitter taste, which is tempered by dry-roasting. Black cumin seeds, which are also known as nigella, are milder and sweeter, and are reputed to have

GRINDING SPICES

Whole spices ground by hand provide the best flavour and aroma. Grind as you need them and do not be tempted to grind too much, as they tend to lose their potency and flavour. Some spices such as mace, fenugreek, cloves, turmeric and cinnamon are difficult to grind at home and are better bought ready-ground. Grind whole spices in a mortar using a pestle – or use an electric coffee grinder if you prefer.

Above: Grated nutmeg enriches the flavour of dishes and aids digestion.

Above: The citral in lemongrass may help to combat cancerous cells.

Above: Mustard stimulates circulation and rids the body of harmful toxins.

anti-inflammatory properties. This is thought to be due to a type of quinone found only in the seed, and has been associated with alleviating joint pain in arthritis.

The flavonoids in cumin do contribute to its antioxidant activity and may have anti-cancer properties. Traditionally, cumin preparations have been used to stimulate digestion and production of bile, helping to alleviate flatulence and indigestion. Ground cumin can be harsh, so it is best to buy the whole seeds and grind them just before use to ensure a fresh flavour. Cumin is good in tomato- or grain-based dishes, and its digestive properties mean that it is also ideal for adding to with beans.

Nutmeg and Mace

When it is picked, the nutmeg seed is surrounded by a lacy membrane called mace. Both are dried and used as spices. Nutmeg and mace taste similar, and their warm, sweet flavour enlivens white sauces, cheese-based dishes and vegetables, as well as custards, cakes and biscuits (cookies). Freshly grated nutmeg is far superior to the ready-ground variety, which loses its flavour and aroma with time. Although it is a hallucinogen if eaten in excess, when consumed in the small quantities that are needed in recipes, nutmeg can improve both appetite and digestion.

Lemon Grass

This long, fibrous stalk has a fragrant citrus aroma and flavour when cut and is a familiar part of South-east Asian and particularly Thai cooking, where it is used in coconut-flavoured curries. Lemon grass contains citral, which gives it its characteristic lemon scent. Citral also shows powerful antioxidant activity and has been shown in research to prevent and reduce cell damage by scavenging free-radicals. This property could have a role in cancer treatments of

PREPARING LEMON GRASS
Remove the tough, woody outer layers, trim the root, then cut off the lower 5cm/2in and slice into thin rounds, or pound in a mortar using a pestle. Bottled, chopped lemon grass and lemon grass purée are also available.

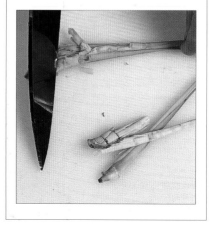

the future. Citral also contains antiseptic, anti-fungal, anti-microbial and anti-inflammatory properties.

Mustard

This spice comes from the fabulous brassica family, and is therefore cruciferous, which accounts for its beneficial value to us. There are three different types of mustard seed, white, brown, and black, which is the most pungent.

The strength of the mustard flavour is totally dependent on how the seed is prepared. Seeds soaked in cold water prior to processing produce the strongest mustards. The characteristic English mustard is made from white and brown seeds and is very strong. Dijon mustard is made from brown and black seeds and is strong. American-style mustard is usually made with a lower level of mustard, is often coloured with turmeric and paprika, and tastes very mild.

The flavour and aroma is only apparent when the seeds are crushed or mixed with liquid. If fried in a little oil before use, the flavour of the seeds is improved. As the intensity of mustard diminishes with both time and cooking; it is best added to dishes toward the end of cooking, or just before the dish is served. Like many hot spices, mustard is traditionally used as a stimulant, cleansing the body of toxins and helping to ward off colds and flu.

Fenugreek

This spice, also known as methi, is commonly used in commercial curry powders, along with cumin and coriander. On its own, however, fenugreek should be used in moderation because its bittersweet flavour, which is mellowed by dry-frying, can be quite overpowering. The seeds contain many active agents such as volatile oils which have been reported to have interesting effects on the body. Fenugreek has traditionally been used to induce childbirth and also to stimulate milk production in breastfeeding women, so pregnant women should be very careful with fenugreek. It has a hard shell and is difficult to grind, but can be sprouted and then makes a good addition to mixed leaf and bean salads, as well as sandwich fillings.

Turmeric

Also a member of the ginger family, turmeric is useful for its yellow colour and earthy, peppery flavour. This intense colour derives from curcumin, a polyphenol which has been the subject of much research in the field of cancer prevention and shows

promising results in the treatment of colo-rectal cancer. Curcumin has also been shown to prevent the formation of plaques in the brain and therefore could slow the progression of Alzheimer's disease; more research is taking place in this area. Curcumin has anti-inflammatory properties; however, robust scientific studies on inflammatory conditions such as rheumatoid arthritis is inconclusive at the moment. Turmeric is mainly available as a powder and only needs to be used in small amounts, as its flavour and colour are so intense.

Paprika

This spice is made from grinding up dried chilli fruit such as the bell pepper or red chilli. It is a milder relative of cayenne and can be used more liberally, adding flavour as well as heat. Like chillies, paprika is very high in vitamin C and contains similar antioxidants. It also contains the stimulating capsaicins, but levels will vary according to the heat of the paprika. This vibrant spice is a digestive stimulant and has antiseptic properties. It can also improve blood circulation, but take care, because if

eaten in large quantities it may irritate the stomach. The chillies are sometimes dried by smoking, and this gives the smoked paprika variety its distinctive taste and aroma. Paprika is used in many cuisines and adds fabulous colour as well as heat and flavour.

DRY FRYING OR TOASTING SPICES
This process enhances the flavour and aroma of spices and is believed to make them more digestible.

Put the spices in a dry frying pan and cook over a low heat, shaking the pan frequently, for 1 minute, or until the spices release their aroma.

Below: The active oils in fenugreek may help to induce childbirth.

Below: The curcumin in turmeric has powerful anti-inflammatory properties.

Below: Paprika contains vitamin C and stimulating capsaicins.

Oils

There is a wide variety of cooking oils and they are produced from a number of different sources: from cereals such as corn; from fruits such as olives; from nuts such as walnuts, almonds and hazelnuts; and from seeds such as rapeseed, safflower and sunflower. They can be extracted by simple mechanical means such as pressing or crushing, or by further processing, usually heating. Virgin oils, which are obtained from the first cold pressing of the olives, nuts or seeds, are sold unrefined, and have the most characteristic flavour. They are also usually the most expensive, but used sparingly they will go a long way.

OLIVE OIL

Indisputably the king of oils, olive oil varies in flavour and colour, depending on how it is made and where it comes from. Climate, soil, harvesting and pressing all influence the end result – generally, the hotter the climate the more robust the oil. One crucial factor remains the same, though; olive oil is rich in monounsaturated fat, which in many studies has been found to reduce

Below: Cook with oil rather than butter as it is lower in saturated fat.

'bad' LDL cholesterol, and its polyphenol content exerts some anti-inflammatory effects as well as keeping blood vessels elastic. Olive oil also contains vitamin E, a natural antioxidant that can help fight off free radicals, which damage cells in the body. All of these contribute to reducing the risk of heart disease and stroke. Characteristic of the Mediterranean diet, populations that consume olive oil as their main source of fat do show a reduced incidence of cardiovascular disease.

Extra Virgin Olive Oil

This premium olive oil has a superior flavour as it comes from the first cold pressing of the olives and has a low acidity – less than 1 per cent. It contains the highest concentration of polyphenols of all the types of olive oil. Extra virgin olive oil is not recommended for frying, as heat impairs its flavour, but it is good in salad dressings, especially when combined with lighter oils. It is delicious as a sauce on its own, stirred into pasta with chopped garlic and black pepper, or drizzled over steamed vegetables.

> **ESSENTIAL FATS**
> We all need some fat in our diet. It keeps us warm, adds flavour to our food, carries essential vitamins A, D, E and K around the body, and provides essential fatty acids, which cannot be produced in the body but are vital for growth and development and may reduce the risk of heart attacks. What is more important is the type and amount of fat that we eat. Some fats are better for us than others, and we should adjust our intake accordingly. It is recommended that fat should make up no more than 35 per cent of our diet.

Above: The lighter in taste an olive oil is, the more it has been refined.

Virgin Olive Oil

Also a pure first-pressed oil, this has a slightly higher level of acidity than extra virgin olive oil, and can be used in much the same way.

Pure Olive Oil

Refined and blended to remove impurities, this type of olive oil has a much lighter flavour than virgin or extra virgin olive oil and is suitable for all types of cooking. It can be used for shallow-frying.

Rapeseed Oil

Also known as canola oil in North America, this is one of the most widely used oils in the world although you may not be aware of it. Many years ago there was a problem with rapeseed oil, where a high level of erucic acid caused an issue. This has since been eliminated and in order to lose the negative associations, the name was not used and rapeseed oil came under the umbrella term 'vegetable oil'. Most vegetable oil labels have the yellow flower of oil seed rape and this is how to best identify it. In a similar way to hemp and flaxseed oils, rapeseed oil also has both essential fatty acids; omega-6 and omega-3 types are present in favourable ratios. It is this ratio that enables rapeseed oil to be included in many commercially produced spreads which are marketed as being an important part of eating a heart-healthy diet, as they reduce the amount of saturated fats we eat and increase the amount of polyunsaturated fats in our diet.

SPECIALITY OILS

As well as the light, all-purpose oils that are used for everyday cooking, there are several richly flavoured oils that are used in small quantities, often as a flavouring ingredient in salad dressings and marinades, rather than for cooking.

Flax Seed Oil

The oil of the flax seed is sometimes more commonly known as linseed oil for wood sealing; however, the food-grade oil is a cold-pressed oil which

---

QUICK IDEAS FOR MARINADES

• Mix olive oil with chopped fresh herbs such as parsley, chives, oregano, chervil and basil. Add a splash or two of lemon juice and season with salt and pepper.

• Combine groundnut (peanut) oil, toasted sesame oil, dark soy sauce, sweet sherry, rice vinegar and crushed garlic. Use as a marinade for tofu or tempeh.

• Mix together olive oil, lemon juice, sherry, honey and crushed garlic, and use as a marinade for vegetable and halloumi kebabs.

---

has not been subjected to harsh solvent extraction processes. The oil no longer contains the lignans or the fibre of the original seed but does still have the vegetarian omega-3 fat alpha-linolenic acid. Flaxseed oil is one of the richest sources of alpha-linolenic acid and contains approximately 50 per cent omega-3 fat. Alpha-linolenic acid undergoes a small degree of conversion to the more bioavailable long-chain omega-3 fats in the body. These have been associated with many health benefits such as reducing inflammation, assisting brain development and function, and also reducing heart disease risk. As for the flax seed, the oil is prone to rancidity and so should be purchased in a dark bottle that does not let light in and should be stored in the refrigerator to prevent degradation. It does have quite a strong flavour, so should be used in salad dressings or to partially replace other oils in a baking recipe. It should never be used as a frying oil as it can catch light easily.

Hemp Seed Oil

Usually cold-pressed for food use, hemp seed oil is a green colour with a subtle nutty, grassy flavour. It contains all of the essential fatty acids in the ideal ratio for the human body to maintain health; these include linoleic acid, an omega-6 fat, and alpha-linolenic acid, an omega-3 fat. Getting this ratio correct is thought to be the key to reducing the incidence of certain conditions. Too much omega-6 fat in our diet may contribute to over-production of inflammatory compounds and exacerbate conditions such as arthritis, high blood pressure and skin conditions. Reducing omega-6 and increasing omega-3 fats may level out this situation and temper the inflammatory response, thus alleviating symptoms. Like flaxseed oil, hemp seed oil should not be used for frying and should be kept in a dark cool place to maximize its

Above: Heart-healthy walnut oil makes tasty marinades and dressings.

shelf-life; it can even be stored in the freezer as it doesn't solidify and doesn't need defrosting.

Walnut Oil

This is an intensely flavoured oil that is delicious in salad dressings and marinades. Walnut oil retains many of the benefits of the walnut. It is an excellent source of the essential omega-3 fats as well as a good source of antioxidants, all of which boost its credentials as a heart-healthy oil.

Walnut oil should not be used for frying, as heat destroys much of the antioxidant activity and diminishes its rich taste (it is also far too expensive to use in any great quantity). Instead, drizzle a little of the oil over roasted or steamed vegetables, use it to make a simple sauce for pasta, or stir into freshly cooked noodles just before serving. It can be used in small quantities, in place of some of the fat or oil in a recipe, to add flavour to cakes and cookies, especially those that contain walnuts. Walnut oil does not keep for long and, after opening, should be kept in a cool, dark place to prevent it from turning rancid. Walnut oil can be stored in the refrigerator, athough this may cause the oil to solidify.

Coffee, teas, tisanes and sweeteners

Coffee, teas and tisanes have been popular reviving and healing drinks for centuries. Tea comes in many different forms, from traditional teas such as green tea, oolong tea and black tea to fragrant tisanes and fruit infusions. Their health benefits have been well documented and used for thousands of years to treat and prevent all manner of illnesses and conditions.

Coffee

There are many compounds in coffee that have an effect on the body, including caffeine, which is a well-known stimulant. Less well known are the phenols that are found in the coffee bean, such as chlorogenic acid. These phenolic compounds have antioxidant properties that are similar to those found in tea and cocoa. The antioxidant activity of coffee increases as the bean is roasted due to the production of other compounds which exhibit antioxidant activity also.

TEA

The latest research shows that drinking between three and five cups of tea a day may help to reduce the risk of heart attack, and it may also reduce the risk of stroke and certain cancers. These benefits have been attributed to a group of polyphenols found in tea, called flavonoids. The type and proportion of the different polyphenols in tea is dependent on how the tea is processed once it has been picked. All of these teas start out life as two leaves and a bud picked from the *Camellia sinensis* tea bush. The longer a tea leaf is allowed to wilt the darker it will become, as it oxidizes in much the same way as an apple goes brown. Hence, black tea is highly fermented and white tea is not fermented at all. As well as flavonoids, tea also contains fluoride, which can protect the teeth against decay. On the downside, tea can reduce the absorption of iron if drunk after a meal, and it contains caffeine (although less than coffee), which is a well-known stimulant.

Black Tea

This is the most widely available tea and is made by fermenting withered tea leaves, which are then dried. It produces a dark brown brew that has a more assertive taste than green tea. It contains fewer epicatechins but a higher proportion of theaflavins and thearubins, both powerful flavonoids that also show anti-cancer activity in cell studies.

White Tea

The difference between white and green tea is the age of the leaf that

Above: Freshly ground coffee beans contain powerful antioxidants.

is picked. White tea is made from the young leaves and bud. The leaves and bud are steamed and dried and there is minimal oxidation, producing a tea very high in catechin flavenoids. These compounds are potent antioxidants which may help in reducing the risk of cancer and heart disease. White tea has a very light and delicate flavour that is described as being slightly sweet.

Green Tea

This tea is popular with the Chinese and Japanese who prefer its light, slightly bitter but nevertheless refreshing flavour. It is produced from leaves that are steamed and dried but not fermented, a process that retains their green colour. Green tea is very high in particular flavonoid compounds called epicatechins, which have been shown to have anti-cancer activity in cell research. This property has yet to be seen definitively in humans. Avoid over-brewing green tea as it will begin to taste bitter.

Oolong Tea

Green tea leaves are bruised and allowed to partially ferment to produce a tea that falls between the green and black varieties in strength and colour. As it is partially fermented, it contains some of the

Below: Black tea is packed full of powerful flavonoids.

Below: Fragrant green tea has high levels of cancer-fighting epicatechins.

epicatechins of green tea as well as the theaflavins of black tea. Fragrant oolong is brewed strong and can have quite a bitter flavour.

Honey

One of the oldest sweeteners used by man, honey was highly valued by the ancient Egyptians for its medicinal and healing properties. The colour, flavour, consistency and quality of honey depends on the source of nectar as well as the production method. In general, the darker the colour, the stronger the flavour. Nutritionally, honey offers negligible benefits, but as it contains fructose, which is much sweeter than sugar, less is needed. Honey still retains its reputation as an antiseptic, having antibacterial properties, and studies show that it is effective in healing and disinfecting wounds if applied externally. This antibacterial activity is thought to work internally also and, when mixed with lemon and hot water, it can relieve sore throats. Do not give honey to children under the age of one year, due to the risk of botulism food poisoning.

HERBAL TISANES

Although herbal tisanes are of little nutritional value, herbalists have prescribed them for centuries for a multitude of ailments and diseases. These teas (made from the leaves, seeds and flowers of herbs) are a convenient and simple way of taking medicinal herbs. They do, however, vary in strength and effectiveness. Shop-bought teas are generally mild in their medicinal properties but are good, healthy, caffeine-free drinks. Even so, some varieties are not recommended for young children and pregnant women and so it is advisable to check the packaging. Teas that are prescribed by herbalists can be incredibly powerful and should be taken with care.

Following is a selection of some of the most popular herbal teas and their properties:

Peppermint tea will release the menthol in its vapours and may help soothe a cold. It is recommended as a digestif to be drunk after a meal.

Raspberry leaf tea may help to prepare the uterus for birth. It is not, however, recommended in early pregnancy.

Rosehip tea is high in vitamin C and may help to ward off colds and flu.

Dandelion and lemon verbena teas are effective diuretics.

Rosemary tea may help stimulate the brain and improve memory and concentration.

Thyme tea freshens the breath and may help with sore throats or coughs.

Elderflower tea is a traditional remedy for colds and fever and an aid to restful sleep.

Camomile tea contains flavonoids and the essential oil bisabolol, and is

FLAVOURED TEAS

Steep your chosen herb, spice or fruit in boiling water and leave to infuse before straining. Peppermint tea is an excellent aid to digestion, and sleep-inducing camomile has a wonderfully calming effect on the nervous system.

To make camomile and peppermint tea, simply mix together 75g/3oz dried camomile flowers and 25g/1oz dried peppermint leaves. Store in an airtight container.

traditionally used to calm the nerves and help to induce sleep. It is also used as a tonic for a sore stomach. Dried camomile flowers have been used for many years to make a soothing herbal infusion. To make your own camomile infusion, use two teaspoons of dried flowers per cup, pour on boiling water and infuse for a few minutes. Camomile is traditionally drunk without milk.

Below: Honey is sweeter than table sugar so you do not require as much.

Below: Camomile tea is renowned for its calming and soothing effects.

Below: Drink elderflower tea before bedtime for a good night's sleep.

Dairy produce

Similar to meat and meat products, this valuable food group has been the subject of much bad press over the years, due to the saturated fat content of its foods. However, eaten in moderation, dairy products provide valuable nutrients such as calcium, which is in its most bioavailable form, vitamin B_{12} and vitamins A and D. Dairy products do provide a complete protein source for vegetarians, and if lower fat options are selected can be consumed as part of a very healthy balanced diet.

Milk

Often referred to as a complete food, milk is one of our most widely used ingredients. Cow's milk remains the most popular type, although, with the growing concern about saturated fat and cholesterol, semi-skimmed and skimmed milks now outsell the full-fat version. Skimmed milk contains half the calories of full-fat milk and only a fraction of the fat, but nutritionally it is on a par, retaining its vitamins, calcium and other minerals. Milk is an important

Below: A daily glass of milk gives you a quarter of your calcium requirement.

source of calcium and phosphorus, both of which are essential for healthy teeth and bones, and are said to prevent osteoporosis. Vitamin D is also present, which is essential for efficient calcium absorption. Milk also contains significant amounts of zinc and the B vitamins, including B_{12}, which is one of the few non-meat products to contain it, and would be a major source for vegetarians.

Bio-yogurt

Produced by the bacterial fermentation of milk, yogurt has been praised for its health-giving qualities and has earned a reputation as one of the most valuable health foods. Yogurt is rich in calcium, phosphorus and B vitamins. Bio-yogurt contains specific bacteria strains such as bifidobacterium which work in harmony with the bacteria naturally present in the intestines to ensure that harmful bacteria do not over-populate. This is reputed to aid digestion and relieve gastrointestinal problems such as bloating. Eating bio-yogurt is thought to be

Below: Creamy, vitamin B-rich bio-yogurt is thought to aid digestion.

> **COOKING WITH YOGURT**
> Yogurt is a useful culinary ingredient, but does not respond well to heating. It is best added at the end of cooking, just before serving, to prevent it from curdling and to retain its vital bacteria. High-fat yogurts are more stable, but it is possible to stabilize and thicken low-fat yogurt by stirring in a little blended cornflour before cooking. Natural yogurt can be used in a wide range of sweet and savoury dishes, and it makes a calming addition to hot stews and curries.

particularly valuable after taking a course of antibiotics as it helps to restore the internal flora of the intestines. There is also evidence to suggest that bio-yogurt containing the acidophilus culture could prevent cancer of the colon. Bio-yogurts, which contain these extra bacteria, have a milder, creamier flavour than other yogurts, and may have far wider healing benefits. Many of these bio-yogurts are also available as yogurt drinks and are a great addition to lunchboxes or picnics.

Eggs

An inexpensive, self-contained source of almost perfect nourishment, eggs offer the cook tremendous scope, whether served simply solo or as part of a dish, whether sweet or savoury. Eggs have received much adverse publicity due to their cholesterol levels. However, attention has moved away from dietary cholesterol to saturated fats, as these have a greater influence on raising the levels of the 'bad' LDL cholesterol, and as eggs are low in saturated fat, they have been somewhat reprieved. They should, however, be eaten in moderation, and people with familial

Above: Eggs are a good source of vitamin B12, choline and iron.

hypercholesterolaemia should take particular care. Eggs provide a good source of B vitamins, especially B12, vitamins A and D, iron and phosphorus, and cooking does not significantly alter their nutritional content. Egg also contains choline, which is vitally important for healthy liver function and is critical in functions such as the metabolism of fats. Choline is also a constituent of acetylcholine, which is an important neurotransmitter in the brain, and has been shown to be deficient in those suffering from Alzheimer's disease.

Omega-3 Eggs
These eggs contain both vegetarian omega-3 and alpha-linolenic acid, and both the animal source omega-3 fats (EPA and DHA). The hens are fed on a high omega-3 diet which includes oily seeds and green vegetation. The hen is able to metabolize this source of omega-3 fats, which are then deposited in the fat of the yolk of the developing egg. This change to the feed of the hens also serves to increase the polyunsaturated fat profile, thus further reducing the level of saturates. This source of long-chain omega-3 fats is particularly useful for vegetarians and those who do not

eat fish or seafood. Eating more omega-3 fats could help our health in many ways, from heart-health benefits through to brain development and protection through to old age.

Cooking with Eggs
Eggs can be cooked in myriad ways. Simply boiled, fried or poached, they make a wonderful breakfast dish. Lightly cooked poached eggs are also filling when served as a lunch dish with high-fibre lentils or beans. Eggs are delicious baked, either on their own, with a drizzle of cream, or broken into a nest of lightly cooked peppers or leeks. They make tasty omelettes, whether cooked undisturbed until just softly set, combined with tomatoes and peppers to make an Italian frittata, or cooked with diced potato and onions to make the classic Spanish omelette. They are also often used as a filling for pies, savoury tarts and quiches.

Eggs are not, however, used only in savoury dishes. They are also an essential ingredient in many sweet dishes. They are added to cake

Below: Poaching eggs is a low-fat way to serve these nutrient-rich gems.

QUICK IDEAS FOR EGGS
• Brush beaten egg on to pastries and bread before baking to give them a golden glaze.
• For a protein boost, top Thai- or Chinese-flavoured rice or noodle dishes with strips of thin omelette.
• Turn a mixed leaf salad into a light supper dish by adding a soft-boiled egg and some half-fat mayonnaise.
• For a simple dessert, make a soufflé omelette. Separate two eggs and whisk the whites and yolks separately. Fold together gently and add a little sugar. Cook in the same way as a savoury omelette and serve plain or fill with jam or lemon curd.

mixtures and batters for pancakes and popovers, are crucial to meringues, whisked sponges, mousses and hot and cold soufflés, and are used in all manner of desserts, from ice creams and custards to rice pudding.

When separated, egg yolks are used to thicken sauces and soups, giving them a rich, smooth consistency, while egg whites can be

whisked into peaks to make soufflés and meringues. It is important to use eggs at room temperature, so remove them from the refrigerator about 30 minutes before cooking.

Buying and Storing Eggs

Freshness is paramount when buying eggs, so it is best to buy from a shop that has a high turnover of stock. You should reject any eggs that have a broken, dirty or damaged shell. Most eggs are date stamped, but you can easily check if an egg is fresh by placing it in a bowl of cold water: if the egg sinks and lays flat it is fresh. The older the egg, the more it will stand on its end. A really old egg will actually float and should not be consumed. It is best to store eggs in their box in the main part of the refrigerator and not in a rack in the door, as this can expose them to odours and damage. The shells are extremely porous, so eggs can be easily tainted by strong smells. Eggs should be stored large-end up for no longer than three weeks.

MISLEADING LABELS

The labels on egg boxes often have phrases such as 'farm fresh', 'natural' or 'country-fresh', which conjure up images of hens roaming around in the open, but they may well refer to eggs that are laid by birds reared in battery cages. It is therefore advisable to avoid eggs that are labelled with such claims and look for 'organic free-range' labels.

HERB OMELETTE

A simple, herb-flavoured omelette is quick to cook and, served with a salad and a chunk of crusty bread, makes a nutritious, light meal. Even if you are going to make more than one omelette, it is better to cook them individually and serve them as soon as each one is ready.

Serves 1
2 eggs
15ml/1 tbsp chopped fresh
    herbs, such as tarragon,
    parsley or chives
5ml/1 tsp butter
salt and freshly ground
    black pepper

1 Lightly beat the eggs together in a bowl, add the fresh herbs and season to taste.

2 Melt the butter in a heavy, non-stick frying pan and swirl it around to coat the base evenly.

3 Pour in the egg mixture and, as the egg sets, push the edges towards the centre using a spoon, allowing the raw egg to run on to the hot pan.

4 Cook for about 2 minutes, without stirring, until the egg is just lightly set. Quickly fold the omelette over and serve immediately on a warm plate.

Meat and poultry

Meat and poultry are often unfairly demonized because of their saturated fat content. However, it must not be overlooked that they contribute significant nutritional value to the diet when prepared and eaten in the right way, and in sensible quantities. Meat and poultry provide valuable, high-quality proteins full of essential amino acids that our bodies cannot make. It also contains the most bioavailable form of iron, as well as zinc and magnesium. Meat and poultry contain a wide array of B-vitamins, including vitamin B12, which is not found in plant-based foods.

The key points to remember are to always choose lean cuts of meat, take off visible fat and skin, and do not eat too much of it. Between 100g and 150g (3¼–5oz) is a more than adequate portion per person. The same rules apply to poultry, and while it is generally lower in fat, taking the skin off can dramatically reduce this from an average of 9 per cent down to only 1 per cent for lean breast meat.

When cooking meat and poultry, try not to add any additional oil or fat, as it often has enough fat to cook in its own juices. To keep the fat content down, grill, stir-fry or bake where possible or use moist cooking methods such as steaming or pot-roasting, which also stop the meat from drying out.

Below: Iron- and vitamin-rich offal is well worth including in your diet.

Grass-fed Meat

It is a well-known phrase that 'you are what you eat' and the same is true of animals. The type of foodstuff used has a dramatic impact on the nutrient profile of animal meat and products. Most animals are either grass-fed, grain-fed or a combination of the two according to the season. When the animals are grass-fed, they are able to produce a far larger amount of a compound called Conjugated Linoleic Acid, or CLA for short, which has been shown to be beneficial to humans. CLA has antioxidant activity and has been shown to have powerful protective effects, helping to reduce atherosclerosis and stimulate the immune system. CLA also changes the way we metabolize fat, and has been shown in some human research studies to reduce body fat and increase lean muscle mass. There has been promising anti-cancer research in the laboratory, which needs more evidence to support a direct link, but most agree that CLAs appear to be beneficial to humans in many ways. The best sources are grass-fed beef and lamb or mutton, organic milk and milk products that tend to be from grass-fed cattle, and eggs.

Chicken and Turkey

Poultry meat is an easily digestible, high-quality source of protein which, with the skin removed, is also low-fat. The breast meat without skin is the lowest fat option at about 1g per 100g, compared with 9g per 100g with the skin. The leg meat is higher in fat at 12g per 100g. The high-quality protein contains essential amino acids that our bodies cannot make, particularly tryptophan. This is a precursor for serotonin, a neurotransmitter, and melatonin, a neurohormone, both of which are involved with sleep patterns and brain activity. It generally has a calming effect, which has led to it being used

Above: Remove the skin to reduce the fat content of chicken meat.

as a sleep aid as well as to help lift moods, and even as an antidepressant. It was once thought that the sleepiness experienced after the turkey-rich meals of Christmas and Thanksgiving were due to the tryptophan levels consumed. However, this is now thought to be attributable to the quantities of food and alcohol consumed.

Offal

There are many internal animal parts that are covered by this definition, however, their use in mainstream cooking is limited, so this book is restricted to the liver and kidney from pigs, sheep and cows, which are much more widely used and readily available. Liver and kidney are excellent low-fat sources of protein and iron, which is in its most available haem (heme) form. They are also an excellent source of vitamins A and B12, riboflavin and selenium, and liver contains choline, which is essential for efficient fat metabolism. They are usually very good value and an excellent meat replacer if you are on a budget. Offal may have gone out of vogue in recent years, but cooked properly, it is delicious, nutritious and well worth trying.

Fish and shellfish

The vast array of fish and seafood available to us nowadays can be quite daunting. To put it simply, fish and seafood can be split into three groups: white fish, oily fish and seafood. White fish is an excellent low-fat source of protein and is easy to digest. Oily fish is slightly higher in fat, but it is a 'good' fat, called omega-3, which we all need to eat more of because of the potential benefits, such as brain and eye development and maintenance and heart health. Seafood is also rich in omega-3 fats and is a great source of protein as well.

We should all be eating two to four portions of fish per week, two of which should be oily, to ensure a good balance of nutrients. Pregnant women are advised to reduce this intake to two portions per week, due to concerns about toxins. However, the benefits of eating fish far outweigh the risks, so it should not be excluded altogether. With global fish stocks dwindling, it is important to try to select sustainable fish sources where possible. The Marine Stewardship Council runs a global certification scheme to show that products have been made in a sustainable way. Approved products can be identified by the 'Blue Tick' on the label.

WHEN BUYING FISH
• For whole fish, always look for bright eyes, a clean smell and bright red gills.
• For fillets or steaks, look for firm clean flesh with no fishy smell.
• For shellfish, look for closed shells or shells that close when touched and feel full, not light.
• Always try to purchase fish as fresh and as near to the cooking time as possible.
• Whether you buy your fish from a supermarket or fishmonger, pre-packed or loose, the same rules apply.

Salmon

Well known as a superfood because it is rich in omega-3 fats, this versatile oily fish is well worth including in your diet. As outlined previously, omega-3 fats are particularly beneficial if you suffer from heart disease, as they can help reduce your risk of further problems. There are many different forms of salmon available and all are worthy sources of omega-3. The richest type is fresh wild salmon due to the omega-3-rich diet the salmon eat in their natural habitat.

Farmed salmon has a good level of omega 3 in it but the feed used is not so rich in omega 3 as the diet of the wild salmon. Smoked salmon and tinned salmon are also good omega-3 sources and these open up a massive repertoire of dishes and meal occasions, from smoked salmon at breakfast through to fishcakes for lunch and risotto for supper.

As well as its fabulous omega-3 credentials, salmon is a good source of other vitamins and minerals, such as B vitamins for energy release, magnesium, phosphorus for calcium metabolism and selenium, which protects the body cells from oxidation. Canned salmon is also an excellent source of calcium, due to the presence of small bones that soften during the canning process, making them safe to eat.

Below: Eat fresh salmon to boost the oily fish quota in your diet.

Above: Trout is a good source of protein, omega-3 fats and B vitamins.

Trout

There are many different types of trout, which are broadly divided into inland trout such as brown trout or rainbow trout, and sea trout, which are brown trout that have migrated to the sea to feed and grow before returning to the river to spawn. Sea trout are generally much larger than inland trout and are very similar to salmon. Inland trout, especially rainbow trout, have a more delicate flavour and texture than sea trout. Both types, however, are excellent sources of protein and B-vitamins and while slightly higher in fat than white flaky fish, it is a 'good' fat containing the essential omega-3 fats. Inland trout is available whole, and can be baked in foil to retain its moisture or as fillets that can be grilled (broiled) in a matter of minutes. It is also available smoked, which makes a tasty alternative to smoked salmon. The larger sea trout is generally available as fillets and should be cooked just as you would salmon.

Tuna

This fish is very popular, primarily due to its ease of use in its canned form. However, while being an excellent protein, niacin and vitamin D and B_{12} source, canned tuna does not have all the benefits of the omega-3 fats found in the fresh fish. This is because the fish is cooked prior to canning to soften the meat, which removes some of the oil, and therefore the omega-3 fat levels are reduced. To get the full omega-3 benefit from tuna, you need to eat the widely available fresh steaks.

There has been much publicity in recent years about fishing practices, sustainability of the species and contamination. Tuna fish shoals often accompany dolphins, probably due to the risk reduction of being attacked by sharks, and this has caused problems when fishermen have used nets; now, line-caught tuna is thought to be safer for the dolphins.

The different types of tuna available have various issues with respect to sustainability and contamination; generally, the larger tuna species, like bluefin, contain the most contaminants, whereas smaller types, such as skipjack, contain the fewest. Nevertheless, all tuna is specifically mentioned as a fish to restrict intake of, especially if you are pregnant, nursing or are thinking of becoming pregnant. For the general population, the benefits of eating tuna in moderation far outweigh the risks and it is to be encouraged.

Herring
This versatile little fish comes in many forms: fresh, pickled, sweet-cured, and kippered, to name a few. It is one of the most abundant types of

Below: Fresh tuna contains far more omega 3 than tinned tuna.

oily fish and its many guises make it an extremely versatile ingredient.

All of the methods of preserving the fish mentioned above tend to retain its nutritious attributes, which include being one of the richest sources of omega-3 fats. It is also a good source of selenium and vitamins D and B12. Many of the preserving methods mentioned use high levels of salt, and so the finished product is high in sodium. It is therefore sensible to eat these sparingly. Herring caught in the Baltic Seas has been known to have high levels of contamination, so try to buy Atlantic, Pacific or Mediterranean herring where possible as contaminant levels will be lower.

Mackerel
Also a very rich source of omega-3 fats, mackerel is another oily fish worthy of mention. Usually very good value for money, this fish is also a good source of selenium and vitamins D and B12.

The whole fish is recognizable by its iridescent silvery-blue skin, with distinctive tiger-like stripes. This fish has been eaten for centuries and the firm, meaty flesh is ideal for grilling (broiling) or baking, the rich flavour perfectly complemented by citrus-based sauces.

Smoked mackerel is also a great source of omega-3 fats and is perhaps more versatile. The fillets can be easily turned into a sandwich filling or a tasty dip, often popular with children, providing a perfect way to include these invaluable nutrients in your family's diet.

Sardines
Who can resist the wonderful aroma of barbecued sardines, reminding us of Mediterranean holidays? The benefits of eating sardines go well beyond the relaxing memories of holidays past; they are another source of omega-3 fats, and the small, thin edible bones also contain calcium, phosphorus and vitamin D in

Above: Oysters are low in fat, yet still contain omega-3 fats and minerals.

significant amounts, all of which are essential to good bone health and the prevention of osteoporosis.

Canned sardines are a cheap alternative to fresh, and retain all of their nutrition, so they make a handy store-cupboard item. For convenience, buy butterfly fillets, which are boned and split open. These can be either marinated or grilled (broiled) with lemon. They cook quickly and need a watchful eye to prevent them from burning.

Oysters
As recently as a hundred years ago, oysters were a staple part of the diet, especially if you lived by the sea or a large river such as the Thames in London. Nowadays, even though oysters are an expensive treat, they pack a low-calorie, nutritional punch. Very rich in vitamin B12, selenium, zinc and iron, oysters are also a good source of omega-3 fats. Their cholesterol content will have little relevance to our blood cholesterol levels, as this is influenced more by the amount of saturated fat that we eat. Oysters are reputed to have aphrodisiac properties and, while this remains unproven, their high levels of zinc and selenium are instrumental in testosterone and healthy sperm production. Freshness is imperative, and oysters should only be eaten or cooked live where the shell will be shut tight.

Index

ACKNOWLEDGEMENTS
Photographers: Peter Anderson, Martin Brigdale, Nicky Dowey, Gus Filgate, Amanda Heywood, William Lingwood, Thomas Odulate, Charlie Richards, Craig Robertson, Simon Smith, Jon Whitaker and Mark Wood.
Picture agencies: Fotalia Page 6bl, 10bm, 21b, 27tm, 28bl, 75tm and 87br.